VOGUE
COTTON &
SILK KNITS

Christina Probert

ANGELL EDITIONS

Newton Abbot, Devon

Acknowledgements

Colour photographs by Mario Testino 4, 9, 15, 49, 54, 57, 58, 64; Perry Ogden 7, 11, 13, 21, 23, 26, 28, 31, 32, 40, 42, 44, 51; Anthony Crickmay 18/9, 36/7, 47, 60/1; Steve Kibble 12. Black and white photographs: Montgomery 17; Ogden 20, 29, 33, 41; Donovan 35, 53, 63; Elgort 55; Hoyningen-Huene 62. Charts by Andy Ingham.

Hair by Pat Lewis for Vidal Sassoon on pages 36/7, 60/1; Kerry Warn of New York 7, 13, 21, 28, 32, 40; Nicky Clarke and Ashley Russell, both of John Frieda 11, 23, 26, 31, 42, 44, 51; Orbie 4, 9; Anthony De May for Glemby 57; Sacha 58, 64.

Make-up by Teresa Fairminer on pages 36/7, 60/1; Mark Hayles 11, 23, 26, 31, 42, 44, 51; Fran Cooper of New York 7, 13, 21, 28, 32, 40; Kevin 4, 9; Leslie Chilkes 15; Jo Strettell 49, 54, 58, 64; Jim Brussock 57.

Hair and make-up by Trevor at Colombe and Arianne on pages 18/9; Pascal 46.

Clothes and accessories by Armani, Laura Ashley, Sheridan Barnett, Basile, Benetton, British Shoe Corporation, Brooks Brothers, Browns, Butler & Wilson, Comme des Garcons, Lawrence Corner, Paul Costello, Courtney, Crolla, Dickens & Jones, Perry Ellis, Fenn Wright & Manson, Fenwicks, Flip, Margaret Howell, Herbert Johnson, Katharine Hamnett, Harrods, Hennes, Herbert Johnson, Hobbs, Joseph, Kenzo, Kir, Calvin Klein, Lana Lino, Liberty, New & Lingwood, Mary Quant, John Marks, Maxmara, Mulberry, Options at Austin Reed, Benny Ong, Maxfield Parish, N. Peal, Andre Peters, Pollen, Marco Polo, Ralph Lauren, Russell & Bromley, The Scotch House, Sacha, Sunarma, Paul Smith, Tessiers, Tatters, Charles de Temple, Patricia Underwood, Whistles, The White House, Walkers, Zoran. International Textile Care Labelling Code courtesy of the Home Laundering Consultative Council.

British Library Cataloguing in Publication Data

Probert, Christina
 Vogue cotton and silk knits. – (Vogue knitting library; 2)
 1. Knitting – Patterns
 I. Title   II. Series
 646.4'304   TT820

ISBN 0-948432-20-9

Printed in the Netherlands
by Royal Smeets Offset, Weert
for Angell Editions Limited
Newton Abbot, Devon

Contents

Elegant, Cotton Evening Blouse

1952

Stocking stitch blouse with deep-ribbed rounded boat neck, set-in sleeves and ribbed cuffs and hem

★★ Suitable for knitters with some previous experience

MATERIALS

Yarn
Pingouin Coton Perle 5
5(5:6:6) × 50g. balls

Needles
1 pair 2¼mm.
1 pair 3mm.
1 circular 2¼mm.–80 cm. (32 in.) long
2 st. holders

MEASUREMENTS

Bust
82(87:92:97) cm.
32(34:36:38) in.

Length
47(48:51:52) cm.
18½(18¾:20:20½) in.

Sleeve Seam
44(46:46:47) cm.
17¼(18:18:18½) in.

TENSION

32 sts. and 40 rows = 10 cm. (4 in.) square over st. st. on 3mm. needles. If your tension square does not correspond to these measurements, adjust the needle size used.

ABBREVIATIONS

k.=knit; p.=purl; st(s).=stitch(es); inc.= increas(ing); dec.=decreas(ing); beg.= begin(ning); rem. = remain(ing); rep. = repeat; alt. = alternate; tog. = together; sl. = slip (transfer one stitch from left needle, knitwise unless otherwise stated, to right hand needle.); cont. = continue; patt. = pattern; foll. = following; folls. = follows; mm. = millimetres; cm. = centimetres; in. = inches; st. st. = stocking st.; one row k., one row p.; g. st. = garter st.: every row k.; incs. = increases; decs. = decreases.

BACK

Cast on 100(108:116:124) sts. with 2¼mm needles.
Work in k.1, p.1 rib for 9 cm. (3½ in.).
Change to 3mm. needles.
Work 4 rows in st. st.
Inc. 1 st. at each end of next and every 6th row until there are 120(128:136:144) sts.
Cont. until back measures 28(29:31:31) cm. (11(11¼:12¼:12¼) in.).

Shape Armholes
Cast off 5(7:8:9) at beg. of next 2 rows.
Dec. 1 st. at each end of every k. row until 104(108:112:116) sts. rem.
Cont. until armholes measure 9(9:10:11) cm. (3½(3½:4:4¼) in.), ending with a p. row.

Shape Neck
1st row: k.42(43:44:45) sts., turn.
Cont. shaping this side:
* Cast off at beg. of next and foll. p. rows 2(3:4:5) sts. once, 4 sts. 4 times, 3 sts. 3 times, 2 sts. twice and 1 st. 6 times.
Work 3 rows.
Next row: dec. 1 st., work to end.
Work 3 rows on rem. 4 sts.
Cast off.
Sl. centre 20(22:24:26) sts. onto holder.
Rejoin yarn to neck edge of rem. sts. and work from *, reading k. for p.

FRONT

Cast on 104(110:116:124) sts. with 2¼mm. needles.
Work 9 cm. (3½ in.) in k.1, p.1 rib.
Change to 3mm. needles.
Work in st. st. as folls.:
Inc. 1 st. at each end of next and every 6th row until there are 128(136:144:152) sts.
Cont. until front measures same as back to armholes.

Shape Armholes
Cast off 6(7:8:9) sts. at beg. of next 2 rows.
Dec. 1 st. at each end of every k. row until 106(110:114:118) sts. rem.
Cont. until armholes measure 6(7:8:8) cm. (2¼(2¾:3¼:3¼) in.), ending with a p. row.

Shape Neck
1st row: work 43(44:45:46) sts., turn, and cont. on these sts.:
** Cast off at beg. of next and foll. p. rows 4 sts. 4 times, 3 sts. twice, and 2 sts. 3 times.
Dec. 1 st. at same edge of every alt. row until 6 sts. rem.
Now dec. 1 st. at same edge on every 4th row until 4 sts. rem.
Work 5(4:3:2) rows.
Cast off.
Sl. centre 20(22:24:26) sts. onto holder.
Rejoin yarn to neck edge of rem. sts. and work from **, reading k. for p.

SLEEVES

Cast on 48(52:56:60) sts. with 2¼mm. needles.
Work 4 rows in k.1, p.1 rib.
Change to 3mm. needles.
Work 8 rows in st. st.
Inc. 1 st. at each end of next and every 8th row until there are 90(94:98:102) sts.
Cont. until sleeve measures 44(46:46:47) cm. (17¼(18:18:18½) in.)

Shape Top
Cast off 6(7:8:9) sts. at beg. of next 2 rows.
Dec. 1 st. at each end of next 5 rows.
Now dec. 1 st. at each end of every k. row until 40 sts. rem.
Cast off 3 sts. at beg. of next 8 rows.
Cast off.

NECK BORDER

Sew up shoulder seams.
With right side of work facing and circular 2¼mm. needle, k. up sts. around neck as folls.: 54(55:56:57) sts. down right back neck, 20(22:24:26) sts. at centre back, 54(55:56:57) sts. up left side, 64(65:66:67) sts. down left front, 20(22:24:26) sts. from holder at centre front and 64(65:66:67) sts. up right front. [276(284:292:300) sts.]
Work in k.1, p.1 rib for 5 cm. (2 in.).
Cast off in rib.

MAKING UP

Set in sleeves.
Sew up side and sleeve seams.

5

Long, Slim, Twenties' Cardigan 1932

Cotton, low-buttoning cardigan with two pockets and set-in sleeves, in wide rib pattern with garter-stitch borders

★ Suitable for beginners

MATERIALS

Yarn
Pingouin Fil d'Ecosse no.5
11(11:12:12) × 50g. balls

Needles
1 pair 2¾mm.
1 pair 3mm.

Buttons
5

MEASUREMENTS

Bust
82(87:92:97) cm.
32(34:36:38) in.

Length (including border)
64(64:65:65) cm.
25(25:25½:25½) in.

Sleeve Seam (including border)
46 cm.
18 in.

TENSION

34 sts. and 40 rows = 10 cm. (4 in.) square over rib patt. on 3mm. needles. If your tension square does not correspond to these measurements, adjust the needle size used.

ABBREVIATIONS

k.=knit; p.=purl; st(s).=stitch(es); inc.= increase; dec.=decrease; beg.=begin(ning); rem. = remain(ing); rep. = repeat; alt. = alternate; tog. = together; sl. = slip stitch (transfer one stitch from left needle, knitwise unless otherwise stated, to right hand needle.); cont. = continue; patt. = pattern; foll. = following; folls. = follows; mm. = millimetres; cm. = centimetres; in. = inch(es); st.st. = stocking stitch; g.st.: garter st.: every row k.

BACK

Cast on 150(156:162:170) sts. with 3mm. needles and work in patt. as folls.:
1st row (right side): k.2(5:8:1), * p.1, k.1, p.1, k.8, rep. from * to last 5(8:11:4) sts., p.1, k.1, p.1, k.2(5:8:1).
2nd row: p.2(5:8:1), * k.3, p.8, rep. from * to last 5(8:11:4) sts., k.3, p.2(5:8:1).

These 2 rows form patt.
Cont. in patt. until work measures 42 cm. (16½ in.) from beg., ending with a 2nd patt. row.

Shape Armhole
Cast off 4 sts. at beg. of next 2 rows, 2 sts. at beg. of next 8(8:8:10) rows and 1 st. at beg. of next 6(8:10:10) rows. [120(124: 128:132) sts.]
Cont. in patt. until work measures 61(61:62:62) cm. (24(24:24¼:24¼) in.) from beg., ending with a wrong side row.

Shape Shoulder
Cast off 7 sts. at beg. of next 8 rows and 7(9:10:12) sts. at beg. of next 2 rows.
Cast off rem. 50(50:52:52) sts. for back neck.

RIGHT FRONT

Cast on 72(75:78:82) sts. with 3mm. needles and work in patt.
1st row: k.1 (edge st.), * p.1, k.1, p.1, k.8, rep. from * to last 5(8:11:4) sts., p.1, k.1, p.1, k.2(5:8:1).
2nd row: p.2(5:8:1), * k.3, p.8, rep. from * to last 4 sts., k.4.
Cont. in patt. until work measures 12 cm. (4¾ in.), ending with a 2nd patt. row.

Work Pocket Opening
Next row: k.1, patt. 25, thus ending with the 3 sts. in rib, cast off next 41 sts. rather loosely, patt. to end. Leave these sts. for the present, on a spare needle.
With spare ball of yarn and 3mm. needles cast on 41 sts. for pocket lining.
1st row: k.8, * p.1, k.1, p.1, k.8, rep. from * to end.
2nd row: p.8, * k.3, p.8, rep. from * to end.
Rep. these 2 rows until work measures 11 cm. (4¼ in.), ending with a 1st row. Cut yarn and return to sts. of right front.
Next row (wrong side): patt. 5(8:11:15), then patt. across sts. of pocket lining, patt. 25, k.1. Cont. in patt. as before until work measures 20 cm. (7¾ in.) from beg., ending with a wrong side row.

Shape Front and Armhole
Dec. 1 st. at beg. of next row then at same edge on every foll. 8th row 8(8:10:10) times, then dec. 1 st. at same edge on every foll. 6th row 13(13:12:12) times.
At the same time, when work measures 42 cm. (16½ in.) from beg., ending at side

edge, begin to shape armhole, while continuing to shape front edge.
Cast off 4 sts. at beg. of next row, 2 sts. at same edge on next 4(4:4:5) alt. rows and 1 st. on next 3(4:5:5) alt. rows.
Now keeping armhole edge straight, cont. with front decs. until all are completed, then cont. straight on rem. 35(37:38:40) sts. until work matches back to shoulder, ending at side.

Shape Shoulder
Cast off 7 sts. at beg. of next row and next 3 alt. rows. Work 1 row, then cast off rem. 7(9:10:12) sts.

LEFT FRONT

Cast on 72(75:78:82) sts. with 3mm. needles and work in patt.
1st row: k.2(5:8:1), * p.1, k.1, p.1, k.8, rep. from * to last 4 sts., (p.1, k.1) twice.
2nd row: k.4, * p.8, k.3, rep. from * to last 2(5:8:1) sts., p.2(5:8:1).
Cont. in patt. as now set and complete as for right front reversing all shapings, including pocket.
Pocket opening row will be worked thus: patt. 5(8:11:15), cast off next 41 sts. rather loosely, patt. to end.

SLEEVES

Cast on 74(74:82:82) sts. with 3mm. needles and work in patt.
1st row: k.8(8:1:1), * p.1, k.1, p.1, k.8, rep. from * to last 11(11:4:4) sts., p.1, k.1, p.1, k.8(8:1:1).
2nd row: p.8(8:1:1), * k.3, p.8, rep. from * to last 11(11:4:4) sts., k.3, p.8(8:1:1).
Cont. in patt. as now set for 4 more rows, then inc. 1 st. at both ends of next row, then at both ends of every 5th row until there are 128(128:136:136) sts., working extra sts. into patt.
Cont. without shaping until work measures 43 cm. (16¾ in.) from beg.

Shape Top
Place marker loop of contrast yarn at each end of last row to indicate end of sleeve seam.
Now work 5 rows straight.
Cast off 1 st. at beg. of next 12 rows, 2 sts. at beg. of next 20(20:24:24) rows, 3 sts. at beg. of next 10 rows and 4 sts. at beg. of next 4 rows.
Cast off rem. 30 sts.

MAKING UP AND BORDERS

Sew up shoulder seams, matching patt.
Sew in sleeves, placing markers level with beg. of armhole shapings.
Sew up side and sleeve seams.

Borders

These are all worked with 2¾mm. needles.

For lower border, cast on 11 sts. and work in g.st. until this strip is long enough to fit around lower edge of jacket.
Cast off and backstitch in place.

For front border cast on 11 sts. and work 10 rows in g.st. then make buttonhole as folls.:

Next row: k.4, cast off 3, k. to end.
On foll. row cast on 3 sts. over cast off sts.
Cont. in g.st., making 4 more buttonholes each 5 cm. (2 in.) above cast-off edge of previous one.

Now cont. in g.st. until border fits all round entire front and neck edges from lower edge of hem border, stretching it slightly around neck edge, to lower edge of other hem border.
Cast off and sew in place.

Make 2 similar strips each long enough to fit around lower edge of sleeve. Sew them in place, joining ends level with sleeve seams.

For pocket borders cast on 7 sts, and work in g.st. until strip fits along cast-off edge of pocket openings.
Cast off, backstitch strips into place.
Slipstitch pocket lining in place on wrong side and neatly sew across ends of borders on right side. Sew on buttons.

Striped Summer Sweater

Stocking stitch sweater in two-colour stripe, with long or short, set-in sleeves, narrow collar and slit front opening

★ Suitable for beginners

MATERIALS

Yarn

Yarnworks Cotton

Short Sleeve Version:
6(7:7:8) × 50g. balls Main Col. A
3(3:3:3) × 50g. balls Col. B

Long Sleeve Version:
7(8:8:9) × 50g. balls Main Col. A
4(4:4:4) × 50g. balls Col. B

Needles

1 pair 3¼mm.
1 pair 4mm.

MEASUREMENTS

Bust

82(87:92:97) cm.
32(34:36:38) in.

Length

61(61:63:63) cm.
24(24:24¾:24¾) in.

Short Sleeve Seam

13 cm.
5 in.

Long Sleeve Seam

42 cm.
16½ in.

TENSION

20 sts. and 28 rows = 10 cm. (4 in.) square over st. st. using 4mm. needles. If your tension square does not correspond to these measurements, adjust the needle size used.

ABBREVIATIONS

k.=knit; p.=purl; st(s).=stitch(es); inc.= increas(ing); dec.=decreas(ing); beg.= begin(ning); rem. = remain(ing); rep. = repeat; alt. = alternate; tog. = together; sl. = slip (transfer one stitch from left needle, knitwise unless otherwise stated, to right hand needle.); cont. = continue; patt. = pattern; foll. = following; folls. = follows; mm. = millimetres; cm. = centimetres; in. = inches; st. st. = stocking st.: one row k., one row p.; g. st. = garter st.: every row k.; incs. = increases; decs. = decreases.

BACK

Cast on 80(86:90:96) sts. with 4mm. needles and A.
Work 4 rows st. st. for hem.
Work in st. st., making stripe patt. as folls.:
6 rows A, 2 rows B, 2 rows A, 2 rows B, 6 rows A, and 2 rows B.
These 20 rows form stripe patt.
Work in stripe patt. until back measures 21 cm. (8¼ in.) from beg., ending with a wrong side row.
Change to 3¼mm. needles and work 10 rows in stripe patt.
Change to 4mm. needles and work in stripe patt., inc. 1 st. at each end of foll. 9th and every foll. 16th row twice more. [86(92:96:102) sts.]
Work straight in stripe patt. until back measures 43 cm. (16¾ in.) from beg., ending with a wrong side row.

Armhole Shaping

Cast off 3(3:4:4) sts. at beg. of next 2 rows, 2(3:3:4) sts. at beg. of foll. 4 rows. [72(74:76:78) sts.]
Dec. 1 st. at each end of next and every foll. alt. row twice more. [66(68:70:72) sts.] **
Work straight in patt. until armholes measure 19(19:21:21) cm. (7½(7½:8¼: 8¼) in.), ending with a wrong side row.

Shoulder Shaping

Cast off 8 sts. at beg. of next 4 rows, then 7(8:8:9) sts. at beg. of foll. 2 rows.
Cast off rem. 20(20:22:22) sts.

FRONT

Work as for back to **.
P. 1 row.

Shape Neck
Next row (right side): k.31(32:33:34), k.2 tog., join in a 2nd ball of yarn and k.2 tog., then k. to end.
Working both sides of neck at same time with separate balls of yarn, dec. 1 st. at neck edge on every 4th row 9(9:10:10) times. [23(24:24:25) sts. each side].
Work straight until armholes measure same as back to shoulder, ending with a wrong side row.

Shoulder Shaping
Cast off 8 sts. at each armhole edge twice, then 7(8:8:9) sts. once.

SHORT SLEEVES

Cast on 56(58:60:62) sts. with 4mm. needles and A.
Work 4 rows in st. st. for hem.
Work in st. st. and stripe patt. as for back, inc. 1 st. at each end of foll. 5th row and every foll. 6th row twice more. [62(64:66:68) sts.]
Work straight in stripe patt. until sleeve measures 14 cm. (5½ in.) from beg., ending with same stripe as back to armhole.

Shape Top
Cast off 3(3:4:4) sts. at beg. of next 2 rows.
Dec. 1 st. at each end of next and every foll. alt. row 10(9:13:12) times more. [34(38:30:34) sts.]
Dec. 1 st. at each end of next 9(11:7:9) rows.
Cast off rem. 16 sts.

LONG SLEEVES

Cast on 40(42:44:46) sts. with 4mm. needles and A.
Work 4 rows in st. st. for hem.
Work in st. st. stripe patt. as for back, inc. 1 st. at each end of foll. 15th row and every foll. 8th row 10 times more. [62(64:66:68) sts.]
Work straight in stripe patt. until sleeve measures 43 cm. (16¾ in.) from beg., ending with same stripe as back to armhole.

Shape Top
Work as for short sleeves.

REVERS

Right Side
Cast on 31(31:36:36) sts. with 4mm. needles and A.
Work 4 rows in st. st. for hem.
Now cont. in stripe patt. as for back as folls.:
Work 2 rows straight.
Next row: cast off 3 sts., k. to end.
Next row: p.
Next row: cast off 3 sts., k. to last 2 sts., inc. in next st., k.1.
Next row: p.
Rep. last 4 rows 4(4:5:5) times more, then first 2 rows once more.
Cast off rem. 3 sts.

Left Side
Cast on 31(31:36:36) sts. with 4mm. needles and A.
Work 4 rows in st. st. for hem.
Now work in stripe patt. as for back as folls.:
Work 3 rows straight.
Next row: cast off 3 sts., p. to end.
Next row: k.
Next row: cast off 3 sts., p. to last 2 sts., inc. in next st., p.1.
Next row: k.
Rep. last 4 rows 4(4:5:5) times more, then first 2 rows once more.
Cast off rem. 3 sts.

COLLAR

Cast on 55(55:57:57) sts. with 4mm. needles and A.

Work 4 rows in st. st. for hem.
Work in stripe patt. as for back but always work 8 sts. at each end of every row in A, (4 sts. for hem and 4 sts. for border).
It will be necessary to use a 2nd ball of A at end of k. rows for border and yarns must be twisted round each other at each change of colour.
Work 18 rows in this way.
Cast off.

MAKING UP

Sew up side, shoulder and sleeve seams.
Set in sleeves.
Sew shaped edge of revers to neck edges of front.
Sew end of collar to back neck and top of revers.
Turn up all hems and sew in position.

Cable-panelled Slipover

1942

Round-necked sleeveless slipover with three cable panels on front and back, stocking-stitch neck and armhole borders, ribbed hem welt

★★ Suitable for knitters with some previous experience

MATERIALS

Yarn
Maxwell Cartlidge Pure Silk
5(5:6) × 50g. balls

Needles
1 pair 2¾mm.
1 pair 3¼mm.
1 cable needle

MEASUREMENTS

Bust
82(87:92) cm.
32(34:36) in.

Length
58 cm.
22¾ in.

TENSION

16 sts. and 19 rows = 5 cm. (2 in.) square

over patt. on 3¼mm. needles. If your tension square does not correspond to these measurements, adjust the needle size used.

ABBREVIATIONS

k.=knit; p.=purl; st(s).=stitch(es); inc.= increase; dec.=decrease; beg.=begin(ning); rem. = remain(ing); rep. = repeat; alt. = alternate; tog. = together; sl. = slip stitch (transfer one stitch from left needle, knitwise unless otherwise stated, to right hand needle.); cont. = continue; patt. = pattern; foll. = following; folls. = follows; mm. = millimetres; cm. = centimetres; in. = inch(es); st.st. = stocking stitch.

FRONT

Cast on 128(136:144) sts. with 2¾mm. needles.
Work in k.2, p.2 rib for 29 rows.
Change to 3¼mm. needles and patt.
1st row (wrong side): p.18(22:26), k.2, * p.16, k.2, rep. from * to last 18(22:26) sts., p.18(22:26).
2nd row: k.18(22:26), p.2, * k.16, p.2, rep. from * to last 18(22:26) sts., k.18(22:26).
3rd row: as 1st row.
4th row: as 2nd row.
5th row: as 1st row.
6th row: k.18(22:26), * p.2, sl. next 4 sts. onto a cable needle and leave at back of work, k. next 4 sts., then k.4 sts. from cable needle, sl. next 4 sts. onto cable needle, leave at front of work, k. next 4 sts., then k.4 sts. from cable needle, p.2, k.16, rep. from *, ending last rep. k.22 in place of k.16.
7th row: as 1st row.
8th row: as 2nd row.
These 8 rows form patt.
Cont. in patt. until work measures 38 cm. (15 in.).

Shape Armholes
Cast off 6 sts. at beg. of next 2 rows, 2(4:4) sts. at beg. of foll. 2 rows, and 2 sts. at beg. of next 5(6:6) rows. [104 sts.] **
Cont. without shaping until work measures 51 cm. (20 in.).

Shape Neck
Next row: patt. 44 sts., cast off 16 sts., patt. to end.
Cont. on first group of sts.
Work 1 row, thus ending at neck edge.
Next row: cast off 2 sts., work to end.

Rep. last 2 rows twice more.
Work 1 row.
Dec. 1 st. at neck edge on next and every alt. row 6 times. [32 sts.]
Work 10 rows without shaping. Cast off 11 sts. at shoulder edge on next 2 alt. rows.
Work 1 row.
Cast off rem. 10 sts.
Rejoin yarn to neck edge of rem. group of sts., and work to match first side, reversing shapings.

BACK

Work as for front to **.
Cont. without shaping until back measures same as to beg. of shoulder shaping on front.

Shape Shoulders
Next row: cast off 11, patt. 23 (including st. on needle after casting off), cast off 36, work to end.
Cont. on first group of sts.
1st row: cast off 11 sts., work to end.
2nd row: k.2 tog., work to end.
3rd row: as 1st row.
4th row: as 2nd row.
Cast off rem. sts.
Rejoin yarn to neck edge of second group of shoulder sts., and work as folls.:
1st row: k.2 tog., work to end.
2nd row: cast off 11 sts., work to end.
3rd row: as 1st row.
Cast off rem. sts.

BORDERS

Neck Border
Sew up left shoulder seam. With 2¾mm. needles, pick up and k.5 sts. at right side of back, 36 sts. at centre, 5 sts. at left side of back, 37 sts. down left side of front, 16 sts. at centre front, 37 sts. at left side of front. [136 sts.]
Work in k.2, p.2 rib for 2 cm. (¾ in.).
Cast off in rib.

Armhole Borders
Sew up right shoulder seam.
With 2¾mm. needles pick up 156 sts. evenly around armhole.
Work in k.2, p.2 rib for 2 cm. (¾ in.).
Cast off in rib.

MAKING UP

Sew up side seams.
Press lightly using damp cloth and warm iron.

Acorn and Eyelet Stitch Sweater

Long- or short-sleeved cotton sweater in patterned bands with reversed stocking-stitch neckband, buttoned back opening and ribbed welts

★ Suitable for adventurous beginners

MATERIALS

Yarn
Pingouin Coton Naturel 8 Fils
Short Sleeve Version:
10(10:11:11:12) × 50g. balls
Long Sleeve Version:
11(12:12:13:13) × 50g. balls

Needles
1 pair 3¼mm.
1 pair 4mm.

Buttons
4

MEASUREMENTS

Bust
82(87:92:97:102) cm.
32(34:36:38:40) in.

Length
57(58:59:60:61) cm.
22¼(22¾:23¼:23½:24) in

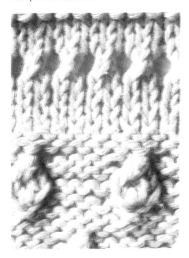

Short Sleeve Seam
19 cm.
7½ in.

Long Sleeve Seam
46 cm.
18 in.

TENSION

21 sts. and 28 rows = 10 cm. (4 in.) square over patt. on 4mm. needles. If your tension square does not correspond to these measurements, adjust the needle size used.

ABBREVIATIONS

k.=knit; p.=purl; st(s).=stitch(es); inc.= increase; dec.=decrease; beg.=begin(ning); rem. = remain(ing); rep. = repeat; alt. = alternate; tog. = together; sl. = slip stitch (transfer one stitch from left needle, knitwise unless otherwise stated, to right hand needle.); cont. = continue; patt. = pattern; foll. = following; folls. = follows; mm. = millimetres; cm. = centimetres; in. = inch(es); st.st. = stocking stitch; y.fwd. = yarn forward; m.1 = make 1 st. by picking up horizontal loop lying before next st. and working into back of it; d.c. = double crochet.

BACK

** Cast on 82(86:94:98:106) sts. with 3¼mm. needles.
1st row: k.2, * p.2, k.2, rep. from * to end.
2nd row: p.2, * k.2, p.2, rep. from * to end.
Cont. in rib until work measures 10 cm. (4 in.), inc. 5(7:5:7:5) sts. evenly across last row. [87(93:99:105:111) sts.]
Change to 4mm. needles.
Now work in patt. as folls.:
1st row (right side): p.
2nd row: k.

3rd row: p.4, * (k.1, y.fwd., k.1) in next st., p.5, rep. from * to last 5 sts., (k.1, y.fwd., k.1) in next st., p.4.
4th row: k.4, * p.3, k.5, rep. from * to last 7 sts., p.3, k.4.
5th row: p.4, * k.3, p.5, rep. from * to last 7 sts., k.3, p.4.
6th row: k.4, * p.3 tog., k.5, rep. from * to last 7 sts., p.3 tog., k.4.
7th row: p.
8th row: k.
9th row: p.7, * (k.1, y.fwd., k.1) in next st., p.5, rep. from * to last 2 sts., p.2.
10th row: k.7, * p.3, k.5, rep. from * to last 2 sts., k.2.
11th row: p.7, * k.3, p.5, rep. from * to last 2 sts., p.2.
12th row: k.7, * p.3 tog., k.5, rep. from * to last 2 sts., k.2.
13th row: p.
14th row: k.
15th to 20th rows: as 3rd to 8th.
21st row: k.
22nd row: p.
23rd and 24th rows: as 21st and 22nd.
25th row: k.1, * y.fwd, k.2 tog., rep. from * to end.
26th row: p.
27th row: k.
28th row: p.
29th to 34th rows: rep. 26th to 28th rows twice.
35th row: as 25th.
36th row: p.
37th row: k.
38th row: p.
These 38 rows form patt.
Rep. these 38 patt. rows once more.

Shape Armholes
Keeping patt. correct, cast off 4 sts. at beg. of next 2 rows.
Dec. 1 st. at each end of next 3 rows, then on every foll. alt. row until 69(71:73:77:79) sts. rem. **
Cont. in patt. until back measures 47(48:49:50:51) cm. (18½(18¾:19¼:19½:20) in.) ending with a wrong side row.

Divide for back opening.
Next row: patt. 34(35:36:38:39), turn and leave rem. sts. on a spare needle.
Cont. in patt. until work measures 57(58: 59:60:61) cm. (22¼(22¾:23¼:23½:24) in.) ending with a wrong side row.

Shape Shoulder
Keeping patt. correct, cast off 7 sts. at beg. of next and foll. alt. row.
Work 1 row.
Cast off 6(6:6:7:7) sts.
Leave rem. 14(15:16:17:18) sts. on a spare needle.
With right side facing rejoin yarn to rem. sts.
Cast off 1 st., patt. to end.
Work to match first side, reversing shapings.

FRONT
Work as for back from ** to **.
Cont. in patt. until front measures 51(52: 53:54:55) cm. (20(20½:20¾:21¼:21½) in.), ending with a wrong side row.

Shape Neck
Patt. 25(26:27:29:30), work 2 tog., turn and leave rem. sts. on a spare needle.
Dec. 1 st. at neck edge on every row until 20(20:20:21:21) sts. rem.
Work straight until front matches back to shoulder, ending with a wrong side row.

Shape Shoulder
Keeping patt. correct, cast off 7 sts. at beg. of next and foll. alt. row.
Work 1 row.
Cast off rem. 6(6:6:7:7) sts.
With right side facing, slip first 15 sts. onto

a spare needle, rejoin yarn to rem. sts., work 2 tog., patt. to end.
Work to match first side, reversing shapings.

SHORT SLEEVES
Cast on 46(46:50:50:54) sts. with 3¼mm. needles and work in rib as on back for 5 cm. (2 in.), inc. 17(17:19:19:21) sts. evenly across last row. [63(63:69:69:75) sts.]

Change to 4mm. needles.
Work 38 patt. rows as on back once only.
Shape Top
Cast off 4 sts. at beg. of next 2 rows.
Dec. 1 st. at each end of next and every foll. 4th row until 47(45:51:49:59) sts. rem.
Work 1 row.
Dec. 1 st. at each end of next and every foll. alt. row until 21 sts. rem.
Work 1 row.
Cast off.

LONG SLEEVES
Cast on 38(38:42:42:46) sts. with 3¼mm. needles and work in rib as on back for 5 cm. (2 in.), inc. 25(25:27:27:29) sts. evenly across last row. [63(63:69:69:75) sts.]
With 4mm. needles work the 38 patt. rows as on back, 3 times.
Shape top as for short-sleeved version.

NECK BORDER
Sew up shoulder seams.
With right side facing and 3¼mm. needles, k.14(15:16:17:18) sts. from left back, k. up 16 sts. down left side of neck, k.15 sts. across centre, k. up 16 sts. up right side of neck, then k.14(15:16:17:18) sts. from right back. [75(77:79:81:83) sts.]
Starting with a k. row, work 8 rows in st.st. Cast off.

MAKING UP
Sew up side and sleeve seams.
Set in sleeves.
Work 2 rows of d.c. round back neck opening, making 4 buttonholes on right side in 2nd row.
DO NOT PRESS. Sew on buttons.

Sleeveless Cotton Twinset 1955

Stocking stitch, sleeveless cardigan with two bands of stripes in contrast colour, bandeau top with matching stripe

★★ Suitable for knitters with some previous experience

MATERIALS
Yarn
Phildar Perle 5
8(8:9) × 40g. balls Main Col. A
1 × 40g. ball Col. B

Needles
1 pair 2mm.
1 pair 2½mm.
1 crochet hook 2½mm.

Buttons
6

Elastic (for bandeau top)
60 cm. approx.
23¾ in. approx.

MEASUREMENTS
Bust
87(92:97) cm.
34(36:38) in.

Length
Bandeau top:
34(35:36) cm.
13¼(13¾:14) in.
Cardigan:
61(62:63) cm.
24(24¼:24¾) in.

TENSION
30 sts. and 40 rows = 10 cm. (4 in.) square over st. st. on 2½mm. needles. If your tension square does not correspond to

these measurements, adjust the needle size used.

ABBREVIATIONS

k.=knit; p.=purl; st(s).=stitch(es); inc.= increas(ing); dec.=decreas(ing); beg.= begin(ning); rem. = remain(ing); rep. = repeat; alt. = alternate; tog. = together; sl. = slip (transfer one stitch from left needle, knitwise unless otherwise stated, to right hand needle.); cont. = continue; patt. = pattern; foll. = following; folls. = follows; mm. = millimetres; cm. = centimetres; in. = inches; st. st. = stocking st.: one row k., one row p.; g. st. = garter st.: every row k.; incs. = increases; decs. = decreases; d.c. = double crochet.

NB When working in stripe patt. carry col. not in use loosely up side of work.

BANDEAU TOP

Cast on 114(122:130) sts. with 2mm. needles.
Work in rib as folls.:
1st row (right side): k.2, * p.2, k.2, rep. from * to end.
2nd row: p.2, * k.2, p.2, rep. from * to end.
Work 7 cm. (2¾ in.) in rib patt., ending with a 2nd row, inc. 2(2:4) sts. on last row. [116(124:134) sts.]

Shape Sides

Change to 2½mm. needles and, beg. with a k. row, work in st. st., AT THE SAME TIME inc. 1 st. at each end of every 10th(11th:13th) row 8(8:7) times. [132(140:148) sts.]
Cont. straight in st. st. until work measures 29(30:31) cm. (11¼(11¾:12¼) in.), ending with a p. row.
Now work 18 rows in st. st. stripe patt. as folls.:
4 rows B
4 rows A
2 rows B
4 rows A
4 rows B
These 18 rows form stripe patt.
Now cont. in A only:
Next row: k.
Next row: p.
Next 2 rows (fold line): k.
Change to 2mm. needles and beg. with a k. row, work 2 cm. (¾ in.) in st. st.
Cast off.

MAKING UP

Press lightly on wrong side, avoiding ribbing.
Sew up side seams.
Fold hem to wrong side at top and sew in position leaving a small gap for threading elastic.
Thread elastic through top, fasten securely, close gap.
Press all seams lightly on wrong side.

CARDIGAN
BACK

Cast on 142(148:158) sts. with 2½mm. needles and A.
Beg. with a k. row, work 11 rows in st. st.
Next row (hemline ridge): k.
Beg. with a k. row, cont. straight in st. st. until back measures 16 cm. (6¼ in.), from hemline ridge row, ending with a p. row.
Work 18 rows in stripe patt. as for bandeau top.
Now work in A only until back measures 37 cm. (14½ in.) from hemline, ending with a p. row.

Shape Armholes

Now work in stripe patt. as for bandeau top, AT THE SAME TIME when back measures 40 cm. (15¾ in.) from hemline, with right side facing, keeping stripe patt. correct, cast off 8 sts. at beg. of next 2 rows.
Dec. 1 st. at each end of next and every foll. row 5(7:9) times.
Now cast off 1 st. at each end of every foll. alt. row until 108(110:114) sts. rem.
Work straight until armhole measures 18(19:20) cm. (7(7½:7¾) in.), ending with a p. row.

Shape Shoulders

Cast off 6 sts. at beg. of next 12(10:12) rows.
Cast off 0(5:0) sts. at beg. of next 0(2:0) rows. [36(40:42) sts.]

Shape Back Neck Facing

Cast on 2 sts. at beg. of next 8 rows. [52:56:58) sts.]
Cast off.

LEFT FRONT

Cast on 52(62:66) sts. with 2½mm. needles and A.
Beg. with a k. row, work 11 rows in st. st.
Next row: k.
Next row: cast on 48 sts., p. to end. [106(110:114) sts.]
1st row: k. to last 24 sts., sl.1, k.23.
2nd row: p.
1st and 2nd rows form patt.
Work straight in patt. as set, AT THE SAME TIME work stripes as on back until front matches back to beg. of armhole shaping, ending with a p. row.

Shape Armhole and Front Facing

Next row: cast off 8 sts., work to last st., inc. in last st.
Work 1 row.
Now dec. 1 st. at armhole edge on next and every foll. alt. row 5(7:9) times in all.

Work 1 row.
Dec. 1 st. at armhole edge on next and every foll. alt. row 4(4:5) times in all, AT THE SAME TIME inc. 1 st. at facing edge on every foll. 4th row from previous inc. until there are 93(96:98) sts.
Keeping armhole edge straight cont. to inc. 1 st. at facing edge on every foll. 4th row from previous inc. until there are 97(105:105) sts.
Work 5(3:5) rows straight.
1st and 3rd sizes only:
Inc. 1 st. at facing edge on next and every foll. 6th row until there are 100(106) sts.
Work 5 rows straight, thus ending with a wrong side row.

Shape Neck

All sizes:
Next row: k.54(53:54), turn and leave rem. sts. on a spare needle.
Dec. 1 st. at neck edge on next and every foll. row until 36(35:36) sts. rem.
Work 1 row.

Shape Shoulder

Cast off 6 sts. at beg. of next and 4 foll. alt. rows.
Work 1 row.
Cast off rem. sts.
With right side facing, rejoin yarn to rem. sts.
Cast off centre 23(29:29) sts. loosely, k. to last st., inc. in last st.
Now dec. 1 st. at neck edge on next and every foll. row 18 times in all, at the same time inc. 1 st. at facing edge on every 6th row from previous inc. until there are 9 sts. on needle.
Keeping neck edge straight, inc. 1 st. on foll. 6th row from previous inc. [10 sts.]
Work 5 rows.
Cast off.

RIGHT FRONT

Work to match left front reversing shapings, working 6 buttonholes, first to come 8 cm. (3¼ in.) from hemline, last to come 3 cm. (1¼ in.) from neck, rem. spaced evenly between.
To make double buttonhole:
1st buttonhole row (right side): k.15, cast off 5 sts., work 7 sts., cast off 5 sts., work to end.
2nd buttonhole row: work across row, casting on 5 sts. over those cast off on previous row.

MAKING UP

Press lightly on wrong side.
Sew up side seams.
Turn up hem and sew.
Sew up shoulders.
Fold front facings to right side.
Sew around neck and to back neck facing, sew tog. at lower edge.
Fold facings to wrong side and catch in position at shoulders.
Work 1 row d.c. around edge of armhole and 1 row of s.c.
Buttonhole-st. buttonholes tog.
Sew on buttons.
Press seams lightly on wrong side.

Belted Crochet-look Sweater

1969

Hip-length, fine sweater with belt, set-in sleeves, in broken rib pattern with doubled-over stocking stitch welts and round neck with shaped, edged collar

★★ Suitable for knitters with some previous experience

MATERIALS

Yarn
Twilleys Lyscordet
14(15:16:17:18:19) × 25g. balls

Needles
1 pair 3mm.
1 pair 3¾mm.

MEASUREMENTS

Bust
82(87:92:97:102:107) cm.
32(34:36:38:40:42) in.

Length
63(64:64:65:65:66) cm.
24¾(25:25:25½:25½:26) in.

Sleeve Seam
47 cm.
18½ in.

TENSION

21 sts. and 27 rows = 9 cm. (3½ in.) square over pattern on 3¾mm. needles. If your tension square does not correspond to these measurements, adjust the needle size used.

ABBREVIATIONS

k.=knit; p.=purl; st(s).=stitch(es); inc.= increase; dec.=decrease; beg.=begin(ning); rem. = remain(ing); rep. = repeat; alt. = alternate; tog. = together; sl. = slip stitch (transfer one stitch from left needle, knit-wise unless otherwise stated, to right hand needle.); cont. = continue; patt. = pattern; foll. = following; folls. = follows; mm. = millimetres; cm. = centimetre(s); in. = inch(es); y.fwd. = yarn forward; y.bk. = yarn back; st.st. = stocking stitch; t.b.l. = through back of loops; m.1 = pick up thread lying between sts. and k.

BACK

Cast on 119(127:135:143:151:159) sts. with 3mm. needles. Beg. with a k. row work 7 rows st.st.

Next row: k. all sts. t.b.l. to form hemline. Change to 3¾mm. needles and work in patt. thus:
1st row: *k.1, p.1, rep. from * to last st., k.1.
2nd row: *p.1, k.1, rep. from * to last st., p.1.
3rd row: as 2nd row.
4th row: as 1st row.
These 4 rows form patt. and are rep. throughout. Cont. in patt. until work measures 43 cm. (16¾ in.) from hemline (or length required to underarm) ending with a wrong side row. **

Shape Armholes

Cast off 4(5:6:7:8:9) sts. at beg. of next 2 rows. Dec. 1 st. each end of next 5 rows, then each end of every alt. row until 95(99:103:107:111:115) sts. rem. Cont. without shaping until armholes measure 16(17:18:18:19:20) cm. (6¼(6½:7:7:7½: 7¾) in.) ending with a wrong side row.

Shape Shoulders and Back Neck

Next row: cast off 10(10:10:10:11:11) sts., patt. across 22(22:24:24:24:24) sts., turn. Complete this side first.
Next row: **** dec. 1 st., patt. to end.
Next row: cast off 10(10:11:11:11:11) sts., patt. to end. Rep. last 2 rows once more. ****
With right side of work facing rejoin yarn to rem. sts., cast off 31(35:35: 39:41:45) sts., patt. to end. Cast off 10 (10:11:11:11:11) sts., patt. to end. Work from **** to ****.

Back Neckband

With right side of back facing and 3mm. needles, pick up and k.40(44:44:48:50:54) sts. round back neck. Beg. with a p. row work 6 rows in st.st.
Next row: k. all sts. t.b.l. to form foldline. Beg. with a k. row work 6 rows in st.st. Cast off.

FRONT

Work as given for back to **.

Shape Armholes and Centre Front

Next row: cast off 4(5:6:7:8:9) sts., patt. across 53(56:59:62:65:68) sts., work 2 tog., turn.
Complete left front first:

*** Dec. 1 st. at neck edge on every foll. 3rd row, *at the same time* dec. 1 st. at armhole edge on next 5 rows, then every alt. row 3(4:5:6:7:8) times.
Keeping armhole edge straight, cont. to dec. 1 st. at neck edge on every 3rd row until 30(30:32:32:33:33) sts. rem.
Cont. without shaping until armhole measures same as back to shoulder, ending at armhole edge.

Shape Shoulder

Next row: cast off 10(10:10:10:11:11) sts. patt. to end.
Work 1 row.
Next row: cast off 10(10:11:11:11:11) sts. patt. to end.
Work 1 row.
Cast off rem. 10(10:11:11:11:11) sts.
With right side of work facing slip centre st. onto holder, rejoin yarn to rem. sts., work 2 sts. tog., patt. to end.
Next row: cast off 4(5:6:7:8:9) sts., patt. to end.

17

Complete to match first side, working from **.

Front Neck Band
With right side of front facing and 3mm. needles, pick up and k.62(62:66:68:70:72) sts. down left side of neck, k. centre st. from holder, pick up and k.62(62:66:68: 70:72) sts. up right side of neck.
1st row: p.60(62:64:66:68:70) sts., p.2 tog., p.1, p.2 tog. t.b.l., p. to end.
2nd row: k.59(61:63:65:67:69) sts., k.2 tog. t.b.l., k.1, k.2 tog., k. to end.
Work 4 more rows in st.st., dec. in same way at each side of centre st.
Next row: k.55(57:59:61:63:65) sts., k.3 tog. t.b.l., k. to end. Beg. with a k. row work 6 rows in st.st., inc. 1 st. at each side of centre st. Cast off.

SLEEVES

Cast on 51(51:51:55:55:55) sts. with 3mm. needles. Beg. with a k. row work 7 rows in st.st.
Next row: k. all sts. t.b.l. to form hemline. Change to 3¾mm. needles and work in patt. as given for back, inc. 1 st. at each end of next and every foll. 7th(6th:6th: 6th:5th:5th) row until there are 89(93:97:101:105:109) sts.
Cont. without shaping until sleeve measures 47 cm. (18½ in.) from hemline ending with a wrong side row.

Shape Top
Cast off 4(5:6:7:8:9) sts. at beg. of next 2 rows. Dec. 1 st. at each end of next 5 rows, then every alt. row until 45 sts. rem. Dec. 1 st. at each end of next 3 rows. Cast off 4 sts. at beg. of next 6 rows. Cast off rem. sts.

COLLAR

Cast on 101(103:105:107:109:111) sts. with 3¾mm. needles.
Work in patt. as given for back, inc. 1 st. at each end of 5th and every foll. 4th row until there are 115(117:119:121:123:125) sts.
Work 3 rows in patt. Cut yarn.

Border
With right side of collar facing and 3mm. needles, k. up 30 sts. along short side of collar, k. across sts. on pin and k. up 30 sts. along other side of collar.
1st row: p.
2nd row: k.30 sts., inc. 1, k. to last 30 sts., m.1, k.30 sts.
3rd row: p.
4th row: k.30 sts., m.1, k.1, m.1, k. to last 31 sts., m.1, k.1, m.1, k.30 sts.
5th row: p.
6th row: k.31 sts., m.1, k.1, m.1, k. to last 32 sts., m.1, k.1, m.1, k.31 sts.
7th row: k. all sts. t.b.l. to form foldline.
8th row: k.30 sts., k.2 tog. t.b.l., k.1, k.2 tog., k. to last 35 sts., k.2 tog. t.b.l., k.1, k.2 tog., k.30 sts.
9th row: p.
10th row: k.29 sts., k.2 tog. t.b.l., k.1, k.2 tog., k. to last 34 sts., k.2 tog. t.b.l., k.1,

k.2 tog., k.29 sts.
11th row: p.
12th row: k.30 sts., k.2 tog. t.b.l., k. to last 32 sts., k.2 tog., k.30 sts.
13th row: p. Cast off.

BELT

Cast on 7 sts. with 3mm. needles.
1st row: p.

2nd row: p. twice into each st. [14 sts.].
3rd row: k.1 t.b.l., * y.fwd., sl.1 purlwise, y.bk., k.1, rep. from * to last st., y.fwd., sl.1 purlwise, y.bk.
Rep. last row until belt measures 117(122:127:132:137:143) cm. (45¾(47¾: 49¾:51¾:53¾:56) in.).

Next row: * k.2 tog. t.b.l., rep. from * to end. Cast off.

MAKING UP

Sew up shoulder and neck border seams, side and sleeve seams using backstitch. Set in sleeves. Fold borders at hemline of lower edge, neck and sleeves to wrong side and slipstitch.
Fold collar border to wrong side and slipstitch. Attach collar to neck edge at slipstitch seam and fold over.

Feather-pattern, Cotton Sweater

Naturally dyed, feather-pattern, cotton sweater in eight toning pastel colours, with drop sleeves and ribbed cuffs

★ Suitable for adventurous beginners

MATERIALS

Yarn
Natural Dye Company Cotton
Naturally dyed cotton yarn in eight different colours sold as a pack including two handmade Dorset buttons, (mail order only). Pack colours vary ac-

cording to dye ingredients: here A = pale lilac, B = dark lilac, C = pale rose, D = medium rose, E = dark rose, F = white, G = cream, H = beige.

Needles
1 pair 2¾mm.
1 pair 3¼mm.

Buttons
included in pack: 3

MEASUREMENTS

Bust
87(92:97) cm.
34(36:38) in.

Length
54 cm.
21¼ in.

TENSION

10 sts. and 12 rows = 5 cm. (2 in.) square over patt. with 3¼mm. needles. If your tension square does not correspond to these measurements, adjust the needle size used.

ABBREVIATIONS

k.=knit; p.=purl; st(s).=stitch(es); inc.= increase; dec.=decrease; beg.=begin(ning); rem. = remain(ing); rep. = repeat; alt. = alternate; tog. = together; sl. = slip stitch (transfer one stitch from left needle, knitwise unless otherwise stated, to right hand needle.); cont. = continue; patt. = pattern; foll. = following; folls. = follows; mm. = millimetres; cm. = centimetres; in. = inch(es); st.st. = stocking stitch.

FRONT AND BACK PATTERN

	Main	Contrast
1st patt.	H	D
2nd patt.	E	G
3rd patt.	C	B
4th patt.	A	F
5th patt.	H	E
	armhole	
6th patt.	B	G
7th patt.	F	D
8th patt.	D	H
9th patt.	G	B

N.B. as marked on chart, 1st and 13th rows of each patt. are worked in F.

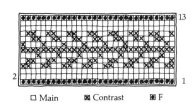

□ Main　☒ Contrast　▣ F

BACK

Cast on 70(76:82) sts. with 3¼mm. needles and E.
Change to 2¾mm. needles.
Work 3 rows each of E, H, A, G, D, F, B in k.1 p.1 rib. (21 rows)
Change to 3¼mm. needles and H.
Work 5 patts. from chart, inc. 15(14:13) sts. evenly across 1st row of 1st patt., and working straight thereafter. [85(90:95) sts.]

Shape Armholes
Cast off 4 sts. at beg. of next 2 rows.
Dec. 1 st. at each end of next row and foll. 5(6:7) alt. rows. [65(68:71) sts.]

Cont. straight until 2nd patt. from beg. of armhole shaping has been worked.
Now inc. 1 st. at each end of next row and foll. 6th rows twice. [71(74:77) sts.]
Work straight until 4 patts. from beg. of armhole shaping have been worked, (i.e. 9 complete patts.).

Shape Shoulders
Cast off 10 sts. at beg. of next 2 rows, 10(11:12) sts. on foll. 2 rows.
Leave rem. 31(32:33) sts. on holder.

FRONT

Work as for back until 2nd patt. after the beg. of armhole shaping is worked, ending with a wrong side row.
Inc. 1 st. at both ends of next row. [67(70:73) sts.]
Next row: p.24(26:28) sts., p.2 tog., p.1, turn.
Dec. 1 st. at neck edge on next 9 rows and at the same time inc. 1 st. on 5th row of armhole edge.
Work 1 row. [18(20:22) sts.]
Inc. 1 st. at armhole edge on next and foll. 6th row. [20(22:24) sts.]
Work 4 rows.

Shape Shoulder
Cast off 10(11:12) sts.
Work 1 row.
Cast off rem 10(11:12) sts., leaving centre 13(12:11) sts. on st. holder.
Work the other front, reversing shapings.

SLEEVES

Cast on 40 sts. with 3¼mm. needles and yarn E.

Change to 2¾mm. needles and work in k.1, p.1 rib as for back and in same col. sequence.

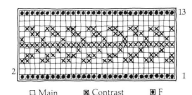

☐ Main   ☒ Contrast   ◼ F

Change to 3¼mm. needles.
Now work 8 patts., inc. 18 sts. evenly across 1st row, and working straight thereafter. [58 sts.]

SLEEVE PATTERN

	Main	Contrast
1st patt.	D	F
2nd patt.	F	E
3rd patt.	B	C
4th patt.	H	D
5th patt.	E	G
6th patt.	C	B
7th patt.	A	F
8th patt.	H	E
	armhole	
9th patt.	B	G
10th patt.	F	D
11th patt.	D	H
12th patt.	G	B

N.B. as marked on chart, 1st and 13th rows of each patt. are worked in F.

Shape Top
Cast off 4 sts. at beg. of next 2 rows.
Dec. 1 st. at each end of next and every foll. 3rd row until 24 sts. rem.
Cont. straight until 4th patt. from beg. of top shaping has been worked, (i.e. 12 complete patts.).
Next row: * p.3 tog.. rep. from * to end. [8 sts.]
Cast off.

SHOULDER RIB

With 2¾mm. needles and F, with right side of work facing, pick up and k.24(26:28) sts. on left back shoulder.
Work 2 rows in k.1, p.1 rib.
Next row: rib 4(6:8) sts., cast off 2 sts., rib 6, cast off 2 sts., rib 10.
Next row: rib across, casting on 2 sts. over those cast off on previous row.
Rib 2 rows.
Cast off.

NECK WELT

Sew up right shoulder seam.
With right side facing and F, pick up and k. approx 86 sts. around neck, using 2¾mm. needles.
Work 5 rows in k.1, p.1 rib.
Cast off.

MAKING UP

Set in sleeves.
Sew up sleeve and side seams.
Very lightly, press seams on wrong side.
Sew buttons on left front shoulder.

Cotton Tennis Sweater

Stocking stitch, V-neck sweater with front and back double cable panels, ribbed welts, and two contrast-coloured stripes in neck welt

★ Suitable for beginners

MATERIALS

Yarn
Phildar Perle 5
10(10:11:11:12) × 40g. balls Col. A
1(1:1:1:1) × 40g. ball Col. B
1(1:1:1:1) × 40g. ball Col. C

Needles
1 pair 2mm.
1 pair 2¾mm.
1 cable needle

MEASUREMENTS

Bust
92(97:102:107:112) cm.
36(38:40:42:44) in.

Length
66(67:68:69:70) cm.
26(26¼:26¾:27:27½) in.

Sleeve
56 cm.
22 in.

TENSION

30 sts. and 40 rows = 10 cm. (4 in.) square over st.st. on 2¾mm. needles. If your ten-

sion square does not correspond to these measurements, adjust the needle size used.

ABBREVIATIONS

k.=knit; p.=purl; st(s).=stitch(es); inc.= increase; dec.=decrease; beg.=begin(ning); rem. = remain(ing); rep. = repeat; alt. = alternate; tog. = together; sl. = slip stitch (transfer one stitch from left needle, knit-wise unless otherwise stated, to right hand needle.); cont. = continue; patt. = pattern; foll. = following; folls. = follows; mm. = millimetres; cm. = centimetres; in. = inch(es); st.st. = stocking stitch; C6F = cable 6 forward: slip next 3 sts. onto cable needle, leave at front of work, k.3, k.3 sts. from cable needle; C6B = cable 6 back: slip next 3 sts. onto cable needle, leave at back of work, k.3, k.3 sts. from cable needle; t.b.l. = through back of loop.

BACK

Cast on 146(154:162:170:178) sts. with 2mm. needles and A, using thumb method.
1st row (wrong side): p.2, * k.2, p.2, rep. from * to end.
Work 8 cm. (3 in.) in k.2, p.2, rib, ending with a right side row.
Inc. row (wrong side): rib 31(34:37:40:43), (inc. 1 in next st., rib 2) 4 times, rib 60(62:64:66:68), (inc. 1, rib 2) 4 times rib 31(34:37:40:43). [154(162:170:178:186) sts.]
Change to 2¾mm. needles and patt.
1st row: k.31(34:37:40:43), p.2, k.12, p.2, k.60(62:64:66:68), p.2, k.12, p.2, k.31(34: 37:40:43).
2nd row: p.31(34:37:40:43), k.2, p.12, k.2, p.60(62:64:66:68), k.2, p.12, k.2, p.31(34: 37:40:43).
3rd row: k.31(34:37:40:43), p.2, C6B, C6F, p.2, k.60(62:64:66:68), p.2, C6B, C6F, p.2, k.31(34:37:40:43) sts.
4th row: as 1st row.
5th row: as 1st row.
6th row: as 2nd row.
These 6 rows form patt.
Cont. in patt. until work measures 44 cm. (17¼ in.).

Shape Armhole

Cast off 8(9:10:11:12) sts. at beg. of next 2 rows.
Dec. 1 st. at each end of every alt. row until 122(126:130:134:138) sts. rem.
Work straight until armhole measures 20(21:22:23:24) cm. (7¾(8¼:8½:9:9½) in.) on the straight.

Shape Shoulders

Cast off 8(8:9:9:9) sts. at beg. of next 4(2:4:6:4) rows.
Cast off 9(9:9:10:10) sts. at beg. of next 4(6:4:2:4) rows.
Work neckband on rem. 54(56:58:60:62) sts.
Change to 2mm. needles and k.2, p.2 rib.
1st row: k.2(3:2:3:2), * p.2, k.2, rep. from *, ending last rep. k.2(3:2:3:2).

Work 2 more rows in A. Break A.
With B, p.1 row.
Work 2 rows in rib. Break B.
With A, k.1 row.
Work 3 rows in rib. Break A.
With C, k.1 row.
Work 2 rows in rib. Break C.
With A, p.1 row.
Cont. in rib until neckband measures 4 cm. (1½ in.).
Cast off in rib.

FRONT

Cast on 146(154:162:170:178) sts. with 2mm. needles and A.
Work 8 cm. (3¼ in.) in k.2, p.2, rib as for back.
Inc. row: rib 58(62:66:70:74), (inc. 1 in next st., rib 2) 4 times, rib 6,(inc. 1, rib 2) 4 times, rib 58(62:66:70:74). [154(162:170: 178:186) sts.].
Change to 2¾mm. needles and patt.
1st row: k.58(62:66:70:74), p.2, k.12, p.2, k.6, p.2, k.12, p.2, k.58(62:66:70:74).
2nd row: p.58(62:66:70:74), k.2, p.12, k.2, p.6, k.2, p.12, k.2, p.58(62:66:70:74).
3rd row: k.58(62:66:70:74), p.2, C6B, C6F, p.2, k.6, p.2, C6B, C6F, p.2, k.58(62:66: 70:74).
4th row: as 2nd row.
5th row: as 1st row.
6th row: as 2nd row.
These 6 rows form patt.
Cont. in patt. until work measures 44 cm. (17¼ in.).

Shape Armhole

Cast off 8(9:10:11:12) sts. at beg. of next 2 rows.
Dec. 1 st. at each end of every alt. row until 122(126:130:134:138) sts. rem.
P.1 row.

Shape Neck

1st row: k.40(42:44:46:48), sl.1, k.1, p.s.s.o., patt. 16 sts., k.3, turn and leave rem. 61(63:65:67:69) sts. on a spare needle.
2nd row: p.3, k.2, p.12, k.2, p. to end.
3rd row: k.39(41:43:45:47), sl.1, k.1, p.s.s.o., patt. 16 sts., k.3.

4th row: as 2nd row.
Rep. 3rd and 4th rows, dec. 1 st. every alt. row as set, at edge of cable panel, until a total of 34(35:36:37:38) sts. rem.
Cont. without further shaping until arm-hole measures the same as back to shoulder, ending at armhole edge.

Shape Shoulder

Cast off 8(8:9:9:9) sts. at beg. of next and foll. alt. rows 2(1:2:3:2) times.
Cast off 9(9:9:10:10) sts. at beg. of alt. rows 2(3:2:1:2) times.
Rejoin yarn at centre front to rem. 61(63: 65:67:69) sts.
Next row: k.3, patt. 16 sts., k.2 tog., k. to end.
Next row: p.41(43:45:47:49), k.2, p.12, k.2, p.3.
Complete to match other side of neck, reversing shaping.

SLEEVES

Cast on 70(74:78:82:86) sts. with 2mm. needles and A.
1st row (wrong side): p.2 * k.2, p.2, rep. from * to end.
Work 10 cm. (4 in.) in k.2, p.2, rib, ending with a wrong side row.
Change to 2¾mm. needles and beg. with a k. row, cont. in st.st.
Inc. 1 st. at each end of 5th and every foll. 8th row until there are 114(118:122:126: 130) sts.
Work straight until sleeve measures 56 cm. (22 in.).

Shape Top

Cast off 8(9:10:11:12) sts. at beg. of next 2 rows.
Dec. 1 st. at each end of every row until 78(80:82:84:86) sts. rem.
Dec. 1 st. at each end of every alt. row until 38(38:38:40:40) sts. rem.
Cast off 3 sts. at beg. of next 6 rows.
Cast off rem. 20(20:20:22:22) sts.

NECKBAND

With 2mm. needles and A, with right side of work facing, pick up 68(70:72:74:76) sts. down left side of neck to centre, pick up 68(70:72:74:76) sts. up right side of neck. [136(140:144:148:152) sts.]
1st row (wrong side): k.0(2:0:2:0), (p.2, k.2) 16(16:17:17:18) times, (p.2, k.1) twice, (p.2, k.2) 16(16:17:17:18) times, p.2, k.0(2:0:2:0).
2nd row: rib 65(67:69:71:73), p.2 tog. t.b.l., k.2, p.2 tog., rib 65(67:69:71:73).
3rd row: break A. With B, p. to end. Cont. in stripes as for back neckband and dec. 1 st. on each side of centre 2 sts. on next and every foll. alt. row as set in 2nd row.
Work until front neckband matches back neckband. Cast off in rib.

MAKING UP

Sew up shoulder and neckband seams.
Sew up side and sleeve seams.
Sew sleeve top into armhole.
Press on wrong side.

Silky Fair Isle Sweater

Fine, silk and wool two-tone sweater with Fair Isle lower body, yoke and cuffs, dotted pattern body and sleeves, and ribbed welts

★★★ Suitable for experienced knitters only

MATERIALS

Yarn
Jaeger Wool-Silk
12(13:13:14:14) × 20g. balls (Main Col. A)
2(3:3:3:4) × 20g. balls (Contrast Col. B)

Needles
1 pair 2¾mm.
1 pair 3¼mm.

MEASUREMENTS

Bust
82(87:92:97:102) cm.
32(34:36:38:40) in.

Length
51(53:57:58:60) cm.
20(20¾:22¼:22¾:23½) in.

Sleeve Seam
43(43:44:44:44) cm.
16¾(16¾:17¼:17¼:17¼) in.

TENSION

28 sts. and 36 rows = 10 cm. (4 in.) square over st.st. on 3¼mm. needles. If your tension square does not correspond to these measurements, adjust the needle size used.

ABBREVIATIONS

k.=knit; p.=purl; st(s).=stitch(es); inc.= increase; dec.=decrease; beg.=begin(ning); rem. = remain(ing); rep. = repeat; alt. = alternate; tog. = together; sl. = slip stitch (transfer one stitch from left needle, knit-wise unless otherwise stated, to right hand needle.); cont. = continue; patt. = pattern; foll. = following; folls. = follows; mm. = millimetres; cm. = centimetres; in. = inch(es); st.st. = stocking stitch; m.1. = make 1 st.: pick up horizontal loop lying before next st. and work into back of it.

N.B. When working in col. patt. from charts, strand yarn not in use loosely across wrong side of work, over not more than 3 sts. at a time, to keep fabric elastic. Read odd rows (k.) from right to left, and even rows (p.), from left to right.

Chart A

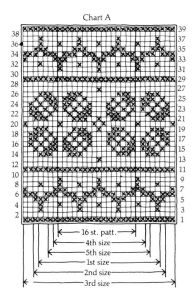

16 st. patt.
4th size
5th size
1st size
2nd size
3rd size

When working col. patt. for main part, carry yarn not in use loosely up side of work.

BACK

** Cast on 116(122:130:136:144) sts. with 2¾mm. needles and A.
Work in k.1, p.1 rib for 7 cm. (2¾ in.).
Next row: rib 3(1:5:3:7), * m.1, rib 5, rep. from * to last 3(1:5:3:7) sts., m.1, rib to end. [139(147:155:163:171) sts.]
Change to 3¼mm. needles and B, and work in patt. as folls.:
***1st row* (right side): * k.1B, k.1A, rep. from * to last st., k.1B.
2nd row: * p.1A, p.1B, rep. from * to last st., p.1A.
3rd row: in A, k.
4th row: p.1A, * p.1B, p.3A, rep. from * to last 2 sts., p.1B, p.1A.
5th row: as 1st.
6th row: as 4th.
7th row: as 3rd.
8th row: as 2nd.
9th row: as 1st.
10th row: in A, p.

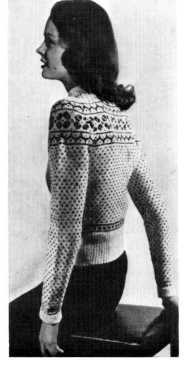

11th row: as 3rd.
12th row: as 10th.
13th row: k.1A, * k.1B, k.3A, rep. from * to last 2 sts., k.1B, k.1A.
14th row: as 10th.
15th row: as 3rd.
16th row: p.3A, * p.1B, p.3A, rep. from * to end. ***
Rep. 11th to 16th rows only until back measures 31(32:35:35:35) cm. (12¼(12½: 13¾:13¾:13¾) in.), ending with a wrong side row.

Shape Armhole

Keeping patt. straight, cast off 6(6:6:7:7) sts. at beg. of next 2 rows.
Dec. 1 st. at each end of next 11(13:15: 13:15) rows.

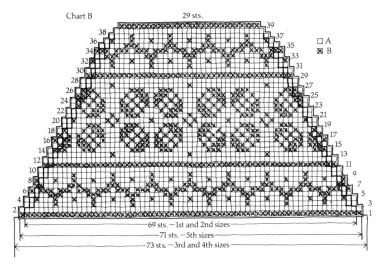

Chart B   29 sts.

□ A
⊠ B

—69 sts. —1st and 2nd sizes
—71 sts. —5th sizes
—73 sts. —3rd and 4th sizes

[105(109:113:123:127) sts.]
2nd, 3rd, 4th and 5th sizes: dec. 1 st. at each end of foll. 1(1:4:5) alt. rows. [107 (111:115:117) sts.]
All sizes: work 1 row, thus ending with a wrong side row.
Now work 39 rows from Chart A, repeating the 16 patt. sts. 6(6:6:7:7) times across, working the first 5(6:8:2:3) sts. and last 4(5:7:1:2) sts. on k. rows, and first 4(5:7:1:2) sts. and last 5(6:8:2:3) sts. on p. rows as indicated.
Next row: in A, p.
Work in patt. as folls.:
1st row: k.2(3:3:3:2)A, * k.1B, k.3A, rep. from * to last 3(4:4:4:3) sts., k.1B, k.2(3:3:3:2)A.
2nd row: in A, p.
3rd row: in A, k.
4th row: p.4(1:1:1:4)A, * p.1B, p.3A, rep. from * to last 5(2:2:2:5) sts., p.1B, p.4(1:1:1:4)A.
5th row: as 3rd row.
6th row: as 2nd row.
Rep. these 6 rows until back measures 51(53:57:58:60) cm. (20(20¾:22¼:22¾: 23½) in.), ending with a wrong side row.

Shape Shoulders
Keeping patt. straight, cast off 10(10:10: 11:11) sts. at beg. of the next 4 rows, then 10(11:11:10:10) sts. at beg. of the foll. 2 rows.
Leave rem. 45(45:49:51:53) sts. on a spare needle.

FRONT
Work as for back from ** until 30th row from Chart A has been worked.

Divide for Neck
Keeping patt. straight, work as folls.:
Next row: patt. 42(43:44:45:45), turn and leave rem. sts. on a spare needle.
Dec. 1 st. at neck edge on every row until 30(31:31:32:32) sts. rem.
Cont. in patt. until front matches back to start of shoulder shaping, ending with a

wrong side row.

Shape Shoulder
Cast off 10(10:10:11:11) sts. at beg. of next and foll. alt. row.
Work 1 row.
Cast off rem. 10(11:11:10:10) sts.
With right side facing, sl. centre 21(21:23:25:27) sts. onto a length of yarn. Rejoin appropriate col. yarn to rem. sts., patt. to end.
Finish to match first side, reversing shapings.

SLEEVES
Cast on 54(54:56:58:58) sts. with 2¾mm. needles and A, and work in k.1, p.1 rib for 5 cm. (2 in.).
Next row: rib 3(3:7:5:5), * m.1, rib 4(4:3:3:3), rep. from * to last 3(3:7:5:5) sts., m.1, rib to end. [67(67:71:75:75) sts.]
Change to 3¼mm. needles, join in B and work in patt. as given for the back from *** to ***.
Cont. in patt. as given for back, shaping

sides by inc. 1 st. at each end of next and every foll. 8th(7th:6th:6th:6th) row until there are 91(95:101:107:109) sts., taking inc. sts. into patt.
Work straight until sleeve seam measures approx. 43(43:44:44) cm. (16¾(16¾: 17¼:17¼:17¼) in.), ending with the same patt. row as on back.

Shape Top
Keeping patt. straight, cast off 6(6:6:7:7) sts. at beg. of next 2 rows.
Dec. 1 st. at each end of next and every foll. alt. row until 69(69:73:73:71) sts. rem.
Work 1 row, thus ending with a wrong side row.
Now work 39 rows from Chart B, dec. 1 st. at each end of rows as indicated on Chart. [29 sts.]
Next row: in A, p.
Cast off loosely.

NECK BORDER
Sew up right shoulder seam.
With right side facing, 2¾mm. needles and A, pick up and k.24 sts. down left side of neck, k. across sts. from centre front as folls.:
k.2(2:3:4:5), (k.2 tog., k.3) 3 times, k.2 tog., k.2(2:3:4:5), pick up and k. 24 sts. up right side of neck, then k. across sts. from back as folls.:
k.4(4:6:5:6), (k.2 tog., k.5(5:5:6:6)) 5 times, k.2 tog., k.4(4:6:4:5). [104(104:110: 114:118) sts.]
Work in k.1, p.1 rib for 7 cm. (2¾ in.)
Cast off loosely in rib, using 3¼mm. needles.

MAKING UP
Sew up left shoulder seam and neck border.
Press according to ball band instructions, omitting ribbing.
Fold neck border in half to wrong side, and slip-hem loosely in position.
Sew up side and sleeve seams
Set in sleeves, matching Fair Isle patt. and easing sleeve top to fit.
Press seams.

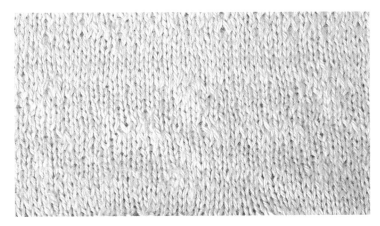

Boat-necked Summer Tunic

Deep boat-necked tunic in broad rib, with three-quarter length sleeves, grafted shoulder seams and dropped armhole

★ Suitable for beginners

MATERIALS

Yarn
Pingouin Fil d'Ecosse 5
8(9) × 50g. balls

Needles
1 pair 3mm.
1 crochet hook 3mm.

MEASUREMENTS

Bust
82–87(92–97) cm.
32–34(36–38) in.

Length
65(67) cm.
25½(26) in.

Sleeve Seam
39(41) cm.
15½(16) in.

TENSION

31 sts. and 36 rows = 10 cm. (4 in.) square over patt. on 3mm. needles. If your tension square does not correspond to these measurements, adjust the needle size used.

ABBREVIATIONS

k.=knit; p.=purl; st(s).=stitch(es); inc.= increase; dec.=decrease; beg.=begin(ning); rem. = remain(ing); rep. = repeat; alt. = alternate; tog. = together; sl. = slip stitch (transfer one stitch from left needle, knitwise unless otherwise stated, to right hand needle.); cont. = continue; patt. = pattern; foll. = following; folls. = follows; mm. = millimetres; cm. = centimetres; in. = inch(es); st.st. = stocking stitch; m.1 = make 1 st.: pick up thread lying before next st., from row below, and k. into back of it.

BACK

Cast on 153(163) sts. with 3mm. needles and work in patt. as folls.:
1st row: p.6(21), * k.1, p.19, rep. from * to last 7(22) sts., k.1, p.6(21).
2nd row: k.6(21), * p.1, k.19, rep. from * to last 7(22) sts., p.1, k.6(21).
These 2 rows form the patt.
Work in patt. until work measures 42(43) cm. (16½(16¾) in.) from cast on edge.

Shape Armholes

Keeping patt. straight, shape armhole as folls.:
Next row: work 1 st., m.1, work to last st., m.1, work 1 st.
Work 1 row. Rep. these two rows once more.
Now m.1 st. at each end of next 7 rows. [171(181) sts.]
Cont. straight in patt. until work measures 13(14) cm. (5(5½) in.) from beg. of armhole shaping, ending with a wrong side row.

Shape Neck

Keeping patt. straight, work as folls.:
Next row: k.65(69) and leave on st. holder, cast off centre 41(43) sts., k. to end.
Work 1 row.
Cast off 3 sts. at neck edge on next and foll. 3 alt. rows, then dec. 1 st. at neck edge on foll. 10 rows. [43(47) sts.]
Work 18(20) rows straight.
Leave these sts. on a st. holder.
Rejoin yarn to armhole edge of sts. for other side, and work to match first side, reversing shapings.

FRONT

Work as for back.

SLEEVES

Cast on 79(83) sts. with 3mm. needles and work in patt. as folls.:
1st row: p.9(11), * k.1, p.19, rep. from * to last 10(12) sts., k.1, p.9(11). ·
2nd row: k.1, m.1, k.8(10), * p.1, k.19, rep. from * to last 10(12) sts., p.1, k.8(10), m.1, k.1.
3rd row: p.10(12), * k.1, p.19, rep. from * to last 11(13) sts., k.1, p.10(12).
4th row: k.10(12), * p.1, k.19, rep. from * to last 11(13) sts., p.1, k.10(12).
Work 3rd and 4th rows once more.
Now cont. working in patt. as set in 3rd and 4th rows, and making 1 st. in manner set in 2nd row, at each end of next row and every foll 6th row, until there are 125(131) sts., working new sts. into patt.
Work 5 rows straight.
Cast off.

MAKING UP AND NECK BORDER

Press all pieces on wrong side.

Graft Right Shoulder Seam

Place front and back with right sides together.

Beg. at end of right shoulder seam with no rem. tail of yarn (neck edge), using crochet hook, take off first st. from holder at front of work onto hook.
Now take off first st. from holder at back of work and draw through the st. already on the crochet hook.
Next take the second st. from the front of the work and draw this through the first st. from the back of work which is on crochet hook, as before.
Cont. in this manner, taking alternate sts. from front and back to end of seam. Cast off by pulling tail of yarn through last st.

Work Neck Border

With 3mm. needles and right side facing, pick up and k. 41(43) sts. down left side of front neck, 41(43) sts. across centre front cast off sts., 82(86) sts. up right side of front neck and down right side of back neck, 41(43) sts. across cast off sts. of centre back neck and 41(43) sts. up left side of back neck. [246(258) sts.]
Turn and cast off.

Graft Left Shoulder Seam

Work as for grafting right shoulder seam. Sew in end left by neck casting-off neatly.

Finishing

Sew cast off edge of sleeve to straight edge of armhole.
Sew up sleeve and side seams.
Press seams.

Stripy Cotton Sweater

Easy sweater in stocking-stitch stripes, with set-in, elbow full-length sleeves, a narrow roll neck and single-ribbed welts

★ Suitable for beginners

MATERIALS

Yarn
Yarn Store Cable Cotton
11(11:11:12) × 50g. balls (Main Col. A)
2(2:2:3) × 50g. balls (Contrast Col. B)

Needles
1 pair 3mm.
1 pair 3¾mm.

MEASUREMENTS

Bust
82(87:92:97) cm.
32(34:36:38) in.

Length
54(54:60:60) cm.
21¼(21¼:23½:23½) in.

Sleeve Seam
40 cm.
15¾ in.

TENSION

23 sts. and 32 rows = 10 cm. (4 in.) square over st.st. on 3¾mm. needles. If your tension square does not correspond to these measurements, adjust the needle size used.

ABBREVIATIONS

k.=knit; p.=purl; st(s).=stitch(es); inc.= increase; dec.=decrease; beg.=begin(ning); rem. = remain(ing); rep. = repeat; alt. = alternate; tog. = together; sl. = slip stitch (transfer one stitch from left needle, knitwise unless otherwise stated, to right hand needle.); cont. = continue; patt. = pattern; foll. = following; folls. = follows; mm. = millimetres; cm. = centimetres; in. = inch(es); st.st. = stocking stitch; m.1 = make 1 st.: pick up horizontal loop lying before next st. and work into back of it.

BACK

Cast on 92(96:100:104) sts. with 3mm. needles and A.
Next row: * k.1, p.1, rep. from * to end.
Rep. this row until work measures 4 cm. (1½ in.).
Next row: k.6(6:5:5), m.1, * k.16(17:18:19), m.1, rep. from * to last 6(5:5:4) sts., k.6(5:5:4). [98(102:106:110) sts.]

Change to 3¾mm. needles. P.1 row.
Work in st. st. in stripe patt. as folls.:
Work 2 rows in B, work 12 rows in A.
Cont. straight until the 6th(6th:7th:7th) stripe patt. has been completed. [Work should measure approx. 30(30:36:36) cm. (11¾(11¾:14:14) in.) from beg.]

Shape Armhole
Cast off 3(4:5:6) sts. at beg. of next 2 rows. [92(94:96:98) sts.]
Cast off 3 sts. at beg. of next 2 rows. [86(88:90:92) sts.]
K.2 tog. at beg. of next 4 rows. [82(84:86:88) sts.] **
Cont. in stripe patt. until armhole measures 20 cm. (8 in.).
Cast off 24(25:26:27) sts., sl. centre 34 sts. onto a holder, cast off rem. 24(25:26:27) sts.

FRONT
Work as for back to **.

Cont. in stripe patt. until armhole measures 16 cm. (6¼ in.).

Shape Neck
Next row: k.29(30:31:32), sl. centre 24 sts. onto a holder, k.29(30:31:32).
Cont. on first group of sts.
Dec. 1 st. at neck edge on every row for 5 rows. [24(25:26:27) sts.]
Work straight in stripe patt. until front measures same as back.
Cast off rem. sts.
Rejoin yarn to other set of sts. and complete as first group, reversing shapings.

SLEEVES

Cast on 48 sts. with 3mm. needles and A.
Work in k.1, p.1 rib as on back for 4 cm. (1½in.).
Next row: k.4, m.1, * k.8, m.1, rep. from * to last 4 sts., k.4. [54 sts.].
Change to 3¾mm. needles, p. 1 row.
Working in stripe patt. as for front and back, inc. 1 st. at each end of every 5th row, until there are 92 sts. Cont. working straight until the end of the 8th stripe. [Work measures approx. 40 cm. (15¾ in.) from beg.]

Shape Top
Cast off 5 sts. at beg. of next 2 rows. [82 sts.]
K.2 tog. at beg. of every row until 46 sts. rem.
Cast off 5 sts. at beg. of next 2 rows. [36 sts.]
K.3 tog. across next row. [12 sts.]
Cast off rem. 12 sts.

NECKBAND

With 3mm. needles and A, k.34 sts. from back stitch holder, pick up and k.16 sts. from first side of front neck, 24 sts. from front stitch holder, then pick up and k.16 sts. from other side of front neck. [90 sts.]
Work in k.1, p.1 rib for 20 rows.
Cast off loosely.

MAKING UP

Pin out pieces, with right side down, to correct measurement and press gently. Darn in and secure all ends of stripe threads neatly.
Sew up shoulder seams and set in sleeves.
Sew up side and sleeve seams.
Join up neck rib neatly.
Press seams.

Cool, Cotton Singlet

1983

Wide-rib singlet with low front neckline, grafted shoulder seam, shaped armholes, and neck and armhole welts in single rib

★ Suitable for beginners

MATERIALS

Yarn
Phildar Perle No. 5
7(8) × 40g. balls

Needles
1 pair 2mm.
1 pair 2½mm.
1 crochet hook 2½mm.

MEASUREMENTS

Bust
82–87(92–97) cm.
32–34(36–38) in.

Length
53(56) cm.
20¾(22) in.

TENSION
36 sts. and 45 rows = 10 cm. (4 in.) square over patt. on 2½mm. needles. If your tension square does not correspond to these measurements, adjust the needle size used.

ABBREVIATIONS
k.=knit; p.=purl; st(s).=stitch(es); inc.=increase; dec.=decrease; beg.=begin(ning); rem. = remain(ing); rep. = repeat; alt. = alternate; tog. = together; sl. = slip stitch (transfer one stitch from left needle, knitwise unless otherwise stated, to right hand needle.); cont. = continue; patt. = pattern; foll. = following; folls. = follows; mm. = millimetres; cm. = centimetres; in. = inch(es); st.st. = stocking stitch.

BACK
Cast on 179(195) sts. with 2½mm. needles and work in patt. as folls.:
1st row: k.4(2), * p.1, k.4, rep. from * to last 5(3) sts., p.1, k.4(2).
2nd row: p.4(2), k.1, * p.4, k.1, rep. from * to last 4(2) sts., p.4(2). Rep. 1st and 2nd rows until work measures 3 cm. (1 in.). Now patt. as folls.:
1st row: k.9(2), * p.1, k.9, rep. from * to last 10(3) sts., p.1, k.9(2).
2nd row: k. all k. sts., and p. all p. sts. Rep. 1st and 2nd patt. rows until work measures 34(35) cm. (13¼(13¾) in.).

Shape Armholes
Keeping patt. straight, work as folls.:

Cast off 10(12) sts. at beg. of next 2 rows. Dec. 1 st. at each end of next 7(8) rows, then dec. 1 st. at each end of foll. 9(10) alt. rows. [127(135) sts.] **
Work straight for 10 cm. (4 in.).

Shape Neck
Keeping patt. straight, work as folls.:
Next row: work 40(43) sts., cast off centre 47(49) sts., work to end.
Work 1 row, leaving rem. set of sts. on a holder.
Cast off 8 sts. at neck edge, then cast off 6 sts. at neck edge on foll. 2 alt. rows, and 4 sts. on 3rd alt. row.
Now dec. 1 st. at neck edge on next 2(4) rows. Work straight for 3(5) rows.
Leave rem. 14(15) sts. on a st. holder.
Rejoin yarn to outside edge of rem. sts. and work other side to match, reversing shapings.

FRONT
Work as for back to **, ending with a wrong side row.

Shape Neck
Next row: work 49(52) sts., cast off centre 29(31) sts., work to end.
Dec. 1 st. at neck edge on the next 25(26) rows, then dec. 1 st. at neck edge on the foll. 10(11) alt. rows. Now work straight for 16(19) rows. Leave rem 14(15) sts. on a st. holder.
Rejoin yarn to shoulder edge of rem. sts., and work to match 1st side, reversing shapings.

MAKING UP AND BORDERS
Omitting ribbing, press pieces on wrong side.

Graft Right Shoulder Seam
Sl. the two sets of sts. onto two spare needles.
With right sides tog., hold needles parallel.
Starting at opposite edge to rem. tail of yarn, take off 1st st. at beg. of front needle with the crochet hook.
Now take off 1st st. from back needle and draw this through previous st. put onto crochet hook.
Take 2nd st. from front needle, draw this through the st. on the crochet hook.
Work in this way, taking sts. from front and back needles alternately, to end of seam.
Cast off by pulling yarn tail through last st.

Neck Rib
With 2mm. needles and right side facing, pick up and k.60(65) sts. down left side of front neck, 29(31) sts. across centre front neck, 92(102) sts. along right side of neck, 47(49) sts. across centre back neck, then 32(37) sts. up left side of back neck. [260(284) sts.]
Work in k.1, p.1 rib for 1 cm. (½ in.).
Cast off in rib.

Graft Left Shoulder Seam
Work as for right shoulder seam.

Armhole Rib
With 2mm. needles and right side facing, pick up and k.190(212) sts. around armhole.
Work in k.1, p.1 rib for 1 cm. (½ in.).
Cast off in rib.

MAKING UP
Sew up side and rib border seams.
Press lightly.

Boat-neck Simple Silk Sweater

Just below waist-length, single rib sweater with set-in sleeves and simple rib neckband forming a placket at front with mitred point

★Suitable for beginners

MATERIALS

Yarn
Maxwell Cartlidge Shanghai
Long sleeved 5(5:5:6) × 50g. balls
Short sleeved 4(4:4:5) × 50g. balls

Needles
1 pair 2¾mm.
1 pair 3¼mm.

MEASUREMENTS

Bust
82(87:92:97) cm.
32(34:36:38) in.

Length
48(48:50:51) cm.
18¾(18¾:19½:20) in.

Long Sleeve Seam (with cuff turned up)
43(43:44:44) cm.
16¾(16¾:17¼:17¼) in.

Short Sleeve Seam
15(15:16:16) cm.
5¾(5¾:6¼:6¼) in.

TENSION

12½ sts. and 16 rows = 5 cm. (2 in.) square over stocking stitch on 3¼mm. needles. If your tension square does not correspond to these measurements, adjust the needle size used.

ABBREVIATIONS

k.=knit; p.=purl; st(s).=stitch(es); inc.= increase; dec.=decrease; beg.=begin(ning); rem. = remain(ing); rep. = repeat; alt. = alternate; tog. = together; sl. = slip stitch (transfer one stitch from left needle, knit-wise unless otherwise stated, to right hand needle.); cont. = continue; patt. = pattern; foll. = following; folls. = follows; mm. = millimetres; cm. = centimetre(s); in. = inch(es); st. st. = stocking stitch.

FRONT

** Cast on 89(95:101:107) sts. with 2¾mm. needles.
1st row: k.2, * p.1, k.1, rep. from * to the last st., k.1.
2nd row: k.1, p.1, rep. from * to the last st., k.1. Rep. 1st and 2nd rows 8 times more.
Change to 3¼mm. needles and st.st.
Work 8 rows. Inc. 1 st. at each end of next row, and then every 8th row until there are 105(111:117:123) sts.
Work until front measures 29(29:30:31)

cm. (11¼(11¼:11¾:12¼) in.) from beg., ending with a p. row.

Shape Armholes

Cast off 4(4:5:5) sts. at beg. of next 2 rows. Now dec. 1 st. at each end of every row until 91(93:97:99) sts. rem., and then every alt. row until 85(87:91:93) sts. rem. ** Work 26(26:28:28) rows without shaping, ending with a k. row.

Shape Neck

Next row: p.27(28:29:30) sts., cast off 31(31:33:33) sts., p. to end.
Cont. on last set of sts. Dec. 1 st. at neck edge on the next 8 rows, and then the 5 foll. alt. rows, ending at armhole edge.

Shape Shoulder

Cast off 7(8:8:8) sts. at beg. of next row.
Work 1 row. Cast off 7(7:8:9) rem. sts.
Rejoin yarn to rem. sts. at neck edge and complete to match first side, working 1 extra row before shaping after last dec. before shaping shoulder.

BACK

Follow instructions for front from ** to **. Work until armholes are 3 rows less than front to shoulders.

Shape Back of Neck

Next row: p.18(19:20:21) sts., cast off 49(49:51:51) sts., p. to end.
Cont. on last set of sts.
1st row: k. to last 2 sts., k.2 tog.
2nd row: p.2 tog., p. to end.

Shape Shoulders

Next row: cast off 7(8:8:8) sts. k. to last 2 sts., k.2 tog.
Next row: p.2 tog., p. to end. Cast off 7(7:8:9) rem. sts. Rejoin yarn to rem. sts. at neck edge.
1st row: k.2 tog., k. to end.
2nd row: p. to last 2 sts., p.2 tog.
3rd row: as 1st row.

4th row: cast off 7(8:8:8) sts., p. to last 2 sts., p.2 tog.
Work 1 row. Cast off 7(7:8:9) rem. sts.

LONG SLEEVES

Cast on 51(51:53:55) sts. using 2¾mm. needles and work 10 cm. (4 in.) in rib as front, ending with first row.
Change to 3¼mm. needles and st.st. Work 4 rows. Inc. 1 st. at each end of next row, and then every 8th row until there are 77(77:81:83) sts.
Work until sleeve measures 48(48:49:49) cm. (18¾(18¾:19¼:19¼) in.) from beg., ending with a p. row.

Shape Top

Cast off 4(4:5:5) sts. at beg. of next 2 rows. Now dec. 1 st. at each end of every row until 59(59:61:63) sts. rem., then every alt. row until 33(33:33:35) sts. rem., and then every row until 19(19:19:21) sts. rem. Cast off.

SHORT SLEEVES

Cast on 67(67:69:71) sts. with 2¾mm. needles and work 10 rows in rib as front. Change to 3¼mm. needles and st.st. Work 4(4:2:2) rows.
Inc. 1 st. at each end of next row, and then every 6th row until there are 77(77:81:83) sts.
Work until sleeve measures 15(15:16:16) cm. (5¾(5¾:6¼:6¼) in.) from beg., ending with a p. row.
Shape top as long sleeve.

MAKING UP AND NECK BORDER

With wrong side facing, pin each piece out to size and shape, omitting ribbing. Press lightly with warm iron and damp cloth. Join right shoulder seam.

Neck Border

With 2¾mm. needles, and with right side of work facing, knit up 23(23:23:23) sts. down left side of front neck edge, 31(31:33:33) sts. from the cast off sts., 23(23:23:23) sts. up right side of neck, and 68(68:70:70) sts. evenly along back neck edge.
1st row: * k.1, p.1, rep. from * to the last st., k.1.
2nd row: k.2, * p.1, k.1, rep. from * to the last st., k.1.
Rep. 1st and 2nd rows 3 times more. Cast off in rib. Sew up left shoulder and neck border seam. Sew up side and sleeve seams, reversing seam on long sleeves for 8 cm. (3¼ in.) from cast on edge. Sew sleeves into armholes. Press seams lightly.

Short-sleeved Silk Sweater

Very simple round-neck sweater with ribbed welts, short sleeves, knitted in stocking stitch

★ Suitable for beginners

MATERIALS

Yarn
Maxwell Cartlidge Shanghai
4(4:5:5) × 50g. balls

Needles
1 pair 2¾mm.
1 pair 3¼mm.

MEASUREMENTS

Bust:
82(87:92:97) cm.
32(34:36:38) in.

Length
48(48:50:51) cm.
18¾(18¾:19½:20) in.

Sleeve Seam
17 cm. (6½ in.)

TENSION

12½ sts. and 16 rows = 5 cm. (2 in.) square over stocking stitch on 3¼mm. needles. If your tension square does not correspond to these measurements, adjust the needle size used.

ABBREVIATIONS

k.=knit; p.=purl; st(s).=stitch(es); inc.= increase; dec.=decrease; beg.=begin(ning); rem. = remain(ing); rep. = repeat; alt. = alternate; tog. = together; sl. = slip stitch (transfer one stitch from left needle, knitwise unless otherwise stated, to right hand needle.); cont. = continue; patt. = pattern; foll. = following; folls. = follows; mm. = millimetres; cm. = centimetre(s); in. = inch(es); st.st. = stocking stitch.

FRONT

** Cast on 89(95:101:107) sts. with 2¾mm. needles.
1st row: k.2, *p.1, k.1, rep. from * to last st., k.1.
2nd row: * k.1, p.1, rep. from * to last st., k.1.
Rep. 1st and 2nd rows 6 times more.
Change to 3¼mm. needles and st.st. Work 8 rows. Inc. 1 st. at each end of next row, and then every 8th row until there are 105(111:117:123) sts.
Work until front measures 29(29:30:30) cm. (11¼(11¼:11¾:11¾) in.) from beg., ending with a p. row.

Shape Armholes
Cast off 4(4:5:5) sts. at beg. of next 2 rows.

Now dec. 1 st. at each end of next row, and then every alt. row until 85(87:91:93) sts. rem. ** Work until armholes measure 13(14:15:15) cm. (5(5½:5¾:5¾) in.), measured straight, ending with a p. row.

Shape Neck
Next row: k.35(36:37:38) sts., turn, leaving rem. sts. on a spare needle. Cont. on these sts., dec. 1 st. at neck edge on the next 7 rows, and then the foll. 3 alt. rows, ending at armhole edge.

Shape Shoulder
Cast off 6(7:6:7) sts. at beg. of next row, and 6(6:7:7) sts. at beg. of 2 foll. alt. rows. Work 1 row.
Cast off rem. 7 sts.
Rejoin yarn to rem. sts. at neck edge.
Next row: cast off 15(15:17:17) sts. loosely, k. to end.
Complete to match first side, working 1 row more, to reach armhole edge, before shaping shoulder.

BACK

Work as for front from ** to **. Work until armholes measure same as front, ending with a p. row.

Shape Shoulders and Back of Neck
Cast off 6(7:6:7) sts. at beg. of next 2 rows.
Next row: cast off 6(6:7:7) sts., k.16(16:17:17) sts. including st. on needle, cast off 29(29:31:31) sts. loosely, k. to end. Cont. on last set of sts.
1st row: cast off 6(6:7:7) sts., p. to last 2 sts., p.2 tog.
2nd row: k.2 tog., k. to end.
3rd row: as 1st row. Work 1 row.
Cast off 7 rem. sts.
Rejoin yarn to rem. sts. at neck edge.
1st row: p.2 tog., p. to end.
2nd row: cast off 6(6:7:7) sts., k. to last 2 sts., k.2 tog.
3rd row: as 1st row.
Cast off 7 rem. sts.

SLEEVES

Cast on 67(69:69:71) sts. with 2¾mm. needles.
1st row (wrong side): * k.1, p.1, rep. from * to last st., k.1.
2nd row: k.2, * p.1, k.1, rep. from * to last st., k.1.
Rep. 1st and 2nd rows 3 times more, and then 1st row once.
Change to 3¼mm. needles and st.st. Work 4 rows.
Inc. 1 st. at each end of next row, and then every 7th(7th:6th:6th) row until there are 79(81:83:85) sts. Work 8(8:7:7) rows.

Shape Top
Cast off 4(4:5:5) sts. at beg. of next 2 rows.
Now dec. 1 st. at each end of next row, then every alt. row until 65(65:67:67) sts. rem., then every 4th row until 49 sts. rem., and then every row until 39 sts. rem.
Next row: (k.2 tog.) twice, * k.1, (k.2 tog.) twice, rep. from * to end.
Cast off.

MAKING UP AND NECK BORDER

With wrong side facing, pin each piece out to size and shape, and omitting ribbing, press lightly with a warm iron and damp cloth.
Sew up right shoulder seam.

Neck Border
With right side of work facing and 2¾mm. needles, k. up 23 sts. down left side of front neck edge, 19(19:21:21) sts. evenly from the 15(15:17:17) cast off sts., 23 sts. up right side of neck and 5 sts. down right side of back neck edge, k. up 34(34:36:36) sts. evenly from the 29(29:31:31) cast off sts., and 5 sts. up left side of neck.
1st row: * k.1, p.1, rep. from * to last st., k.1.
2nd row: k.2, * p.1, k.1, rep. from * to last st., k.1.
Rep. 1st and 2nd rows 3 times more, and then 1st row once.
Cast off in rib.
Sew up left shoulder and neck border seam. Sew up side and sleeve seams.
Sew sleeves into armholes.
Press seams lightly.

Fine Silk Roll-collar Sweater

Plain sweater in stocking stitch with raglan sleeves, narrow roll collar and ribbed welts

★ Suitable for beginners

MATERIALS

Yarn
Maxwell Cartlidge Lotus Silk 4 ply
12(12:13:14:14) × 40g. hanks

Needles
1 pair 2¾mm.
1 pair 3¼mm.

MEASUREMENTS

Chest
97(102:107:112:117) cm.
38(40:42:44:46) in.

Length
59(61:63:65:66) cm.
23¼(24:24¾:25½:26) in.

Sleeve Seam
51(52:54:54:54) cm.
20(20½:21¼:21¼:21¼) in.

TENSION

27 sts. and 40 rows = 10 cm. (4 in.) square over st. st. on 3¼mm. needles. If your tension square does not correspond to these measurements, adjust the needle size used.

ABBREVIATIONS

k.=knit; p.=purl; st(s).=stitch(es); inc.= increas(ing); dec.=decreas(ing); beg.= begin(ning); rem. = remain(ing); rep. = repeat; alt. = alternate; tog. = together; sl. = slip (transfer one stitch from left needle, knitwise unless otherwise stated, to right hand needle.); cont.,= continue; patt. = pattern; foll. = following; folls. = follows; mm. = millimetres; cm. = centimetres; in. = inches; st. st. = stocking st.: one row k., one row p.; g. st. = garter st.: every row k.; incs. = increases; decs. = decreases; t.b.l. = through back of loops.

BACK

Cast on 126(134:142:150:158) sts. with 2¾mm. needles.
Work 13 cm. (5 in.) in k.2 t.b.l., p.2 rib patt., inc. 6 sts. evenly across last row. [132(140:148:156:164) sts.]
Change to 3¼mm. needles and st. st.
Work 18 rows.
Inc. 1 st. at each end of next and every 10th row until there are 140(148:154:162: 168) sts.
Work straight until back measures 36(37: 38:40:40) cm. (14(14½:15:15¾:15¾) in.), ending with a p. row

Shape Raglans

Cast off 1(2:3:4:5) sts. at beg. of next 2 rows. *
Dec. 1 st. at each end of every k. row until 48(50:52:54:56) sts. rem.
P. 1 row.
Leave sts. on a st. holder.

FRONT

Work as for back to *.
Dec. 1 st. at each end of next 10 rows.
Now dec. 1 st. at each end of every k. row until 52(54:56:58:60) sts. rem., ending with a p. row.

Shape Neck

1st row: k.2 tog., k.5, turn.
Cont. on these sts. only for first side.
2nd row: p.2 tog., p.4.
3rd row: k.2 tog., k.1, k.2 tog.
4th row: p.2 tog., p.1.
K.2 tog. and fasten off.
Sl. centre 38(40:42:44:46) sts. onto a st. holder, rejoin yarn to inner end of rem. sts. and complete to match first side, reversing shapings.

RIGHT SLEEVE

Cast on 54(58:58:62:62) sts. with 2¾mm. needles.
Work 10 cm. (4 in.) in k.2 t.b.l., p.2 rib patt., inc. 6 sts. evenly across last row. [60(64:64:68:68) sts.]

Change to 3¼mm. needles and st. st.
Inc. 1 st. at each end of next and every foll. 6th(6th:5th:5th:5th) row until there are 110(116:122:128:134) sts.
Work straight until sleeve measures 51(52:54:54:54) cm. (20(20½:21¼:21¼: 21¼) in.), ending with a p. row.

Shape Top

Cast off 1(2:3:4:5) sts. at beg. of next 2 rows.
Dec. 1 st. at each end of every k. row until 28(28:30:30:32) sts. rem., ending with a p. row.
Next row: cast off 4 sts., k. to last 2 sts., k.2 tog.
Next row: p.
Rep. last 2 rows 4 more times.
Cast off rem. 3(3:5:5:7) sts.

LEFT SLEEVE

Work as for right sleeve, reading k. for p. and p. for k. when shaping sleeve top.

COLLAR

Sew up raglan seams, leaving left back raglan sleeve open.
With right side of work facing, and 2¾mm. needles, pick up and k.16(16:16: 18:18) sts. across top left sleeve shaping, 5 sts. down left front neck shaping, 38(40: 42:44:46) sts. from front st. holder, 5 sts. up right front neck shaping, 16(16:16:18: 18) sts. across top right sleeve shaping and 48(50:52:54:56) sts. from back st. holder. [128(132:136:144:148) sts.]
Work 12 cm. (4¾ in.) in k.2 t.b.l., p.2 rib patt.
Cast off loosely in rib with 3¼mm. needles.

MAKING UP

Sew up side, sleeve, and left back raglan seams.
Turn up cuffs and turn over collar to wrong side, sl. st. loosely in place.

Thick Cotton Sweater

Loose T-shape, stocking-stitch sweater in two broad bands of colour, with grafted shoulder seam and ribbed hem welt

★ Suitable for beginners

MATERIALS

Yarn
Pingouin Coton Naturel 8 Fils
9(10) × 50g. balls in A (lower col.)
7(8) × 50g. balls in B (top col.)

Needles
1 pair 3¼mm.
1 pair 4mm.
1 crochet hook 4mm.

MEASUREMENTS

Bust
82–87(92–97) cm.
32–34(36–38) in.

Length
66(69) cm.
26(27) in.

Sleeve Seam
26(28) cm.
10¼(11) in.

TENSION

22 sts. and 28 rows = 10 cm. (4 in.) square over st.st. on 4mm. needles. If your tension square does not correspond to these measurements, adjust the needle size used.

ABBREVIATIONS

k.=knit; p.=purl; st(s).=stitch(es); inc.= increase; dec.=decrease; beg.=begin(ning); rem. = remain(ing); rep. = repeat; alt. = alternate; tog. = together; sl. = slip stitch (transfer one stitch from left needle, knitwise unless otherwise stated, to right hand needle.); cont. = continue; patt. = pattern; foll. = following; folls. = follows; mm. = millimetres; cm. = centimetres; in. = inch(es); st.st. = stocking stitch; m.1 = make 1 st.: pick up the horizontal loop lying before next st. and k. into the back of it.

BACK

Cast on 121(125) sts. with 3¼mm. needles and A.
Work 8 cm. (3¼ in.) in k.1, p.1 rib, ending with wrong side facing.

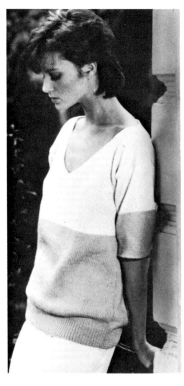

Change to 4mm. needles and dec. as folls.:
1st row: * k.7, k.2 tog., rep. from * to last 4(8) sts., k.4(8). [108(112) sts.]
2nd row: p. to end.
Cont. to work in st.st. until work measures 33(35) cm. (13(13¾) in.) from cast-on edge. Change to B and work in st.st. for a further 13 cm. (5 in.).

Shape Neck
With right side facing, work as folls.:
K.53(55), cast off centre 2 sts., k. to end.
Leave rem. sts. on a st. holder.
Dec. 1 st. at neck edge on the next 11(13) rows, then dec. 1 st. at neck edge on the foll. 22 alt. rows.
Work 1 row.
Leave 20 shoulder sts. on a st. holder.
Work other side to match first side.

FRONT

Work as for back, changing to B 33(35) cm. (13(13¾) in.) from cast on edge, and cont. to work straight until work measures 66(69) cm. (26(27) in.) from cast-on edge.

Shape Neck
With right side facing, work as folls.:
K.20, cast off centre 68(72) sts., work to end.
Leave each group of rem. 20 sts. on holder.

SLEEVES

Cast on 84(88) sts. with 4mm. needles and A. Work in st.st., and change to B when work measures 10 cm. (4 in.) from cast-on edge. Now inc. 1 at each end of first and every foll. 8th row until there are 100(106) sts. Cast off.

FINISHING

Omitting ribbing, press pieces on wrong side.

Right Shoulder Seam
Holding front and back of shoulder with right sides tog., and needles parallel, work as folls.: beg. at opposite side to rem. tail of yarn, take first st. from needle of front onto crochet hook, then take first st. from back needle and draw this st. through first st. on hook. Now take 2nd st. from front needle and draw this through st. on crochet hook, as before.
Rep. to end of sts., pulling tail of yarn through last st. to cast off.

Neck Border
With 4mm. needles and B, right side facing, pick up and k. 68(72) sts. across front neck, 57(59) sts. down right side, then 57(59) sts. up left side of back neck. [182(190) sts.]
Turn work and cast off on next row.

Left Shoulder Seam
Work as for right shoulder seam.

MAKING UP

Sew cast off edge of sleeve to body by positioning centre top of sleeve to shoulder seamline.
Sew up sleeve and side seams.
Press seam.

Cotton Epaulet Sweater

Classic, round-neck sweater in stocking stitch, with ribbed welts, garter-stitch stripes on sleeves and shoulders giving an epaulet effect

★ Suitable for beginners

MATERIALS

Yarn
Rowan Cotton DK
7 × 50g. balls

Needles
1 pair 3mm.
1 pair 3¾mm.

MEASUREMENTS

Bust
92 cm.
36 in.

Length
51 cm.
20 in.

Sleeve Seam
43 cm.
16¾ in.

TENSION

11 sts. and 15 rows = 5 cm. (2 in.) square over st.st. on 3¾mm. needles. If your tension square does not correspond to these measurements, adjust the needle size used.

ABBREVIATIONS

k. = knit; p. = purl; st(s). = stitch(es); inc. = increase; dec. = decrease; beg. = begin(ning); rem. = remain(ing); rep. = repeat; alt. = alternate; tog. = together; sl. = slip stitch (transfer one stitch from left needle, knitwise unless otherwise stated, to right hand needle.); cont. = continue; patt. = pattern; foll. = following; folls. = follows; mm. = millimetres; cm. = centimetres; in. = inch(es); st.st. = stocking stitch; g.st. = garter st.: every row k.

BACK

Cast on 120 sts. with 3mm. needles.
Work 6 cm. (2¼ in.) in k.2, p.2 rib.
Change to 3¾mm. needles and st.st.
Cont. until work measures 33 cm. (13 in.).

Shape Armholes

Cast off 6 sts. at beg. of next 2 rows.
Dec. 1 st. at each end of every alt. row until 92 sts. rem. **

Cont. in st.st. until armhole measures 18 cm. (7 in.)

Shape Shoulders

Cast off 8 sts. at beg. of next 4 rows, 7 sts. at beg. of next 2 rows, then 6 sts. at beg. of foll. 2 rows.
Leave rem. sts. on spare needle or st. holder for neckband.

FRONT

Work as for back to **.
Cont. in st.st. until armhole measures 13 cm. (5 in.).

Shape Neck

Next row: k.35, leave next 22 sts. on a spare needle or holder for neckband, and rem. 35 sts. on another holder or spare needle for other side.
Cont. on first set of sts.

Work 1 row, then dec. 1 st. at neck edge on every alt. row 6 times.
Work 1 row.
Cast off 8 sts. at beg. of next and foll. alt. row. Work 1 row. Cast off.
Rejoin yarn to sts. left for other side and work 2 rows.
Dec. 1 st. at neck edge on every alt. row 6 times.
Work 1 row. Cast off 8 sts. at beg. of next and foll. alt. row. Work 1 row. Cast off.

SLEEVES

Cast on 56 sts. with 3mm. needles.
Work in k.2, p.2 rib for 5 cm. (2 in.).
Change to 3¾mm. needles.
Work 8 rows in st.st. Work 4 rows in g.st. These 12 rows form the patt.
Cont. in patt., inc. 1 st. at each end of 5th and every foll. 6th row until there are 98 sts., incorporating extra sts. into patt.
Cont. straight until work measures 43 cm. (16¾ in.).

Shape Top and Epaulet

Cast off 6 sts. at beg. of next 2 rows.
Dec. 1 st. at each end of every alt. row until there are 54 sts.
Dec. 1 st. at each end of every row until there are 20 sts.
Work 12 cm. (4¾ in.) on these sts., for epaulet.
Leave sts. on st. holder or spare needle for neckband.

NECKBAND

Sew sleeve epaulets along back and front shoulders, leaving left back epaulet open. With 3mm. needles pick up and k.20 sts. of left epaulet (on spare needle or holder), pick up 12 sts. down left side of front, k.22 sts. of centre front (on spare needle or holder), pick up and k.12 sts. up right side of front, k.20 sts. of right epaulet (on spare needle or holder), and 34 sts. of back (on spare needle or holder). [120 sts.]
Work in k.2 p.2 rib for 2 cm. (¾ in.)
Cast off in rib.

MAKING UP

Sew up left back epaulet.
Sew up side and sleeve seams.
Set in sleeves.
DO NOT PRESS.

Mini-check Summer Sweater

Long, roomy sweater with three-colour, slipped-stitch check pattern, set-in sleeves, ribbed cuffs, lower edge, and doubled-over hemmed neck

★★ Suitable for knitters with some previous experience

MATERIALS

Yarn
Phildar Perle 5
6(7:7:7:8:8) × 40g. balls Col. A
3(4:4:4:5:5) × 40g. balls Col. B
3(4:4:4:5:5) × 40g. balls Col. C

Needles
1 pair 2mm.
1 pair 2¾mm.
1 set of 4 double-pointed 2mm.

MEASUREMENTS

Chest
92(97:102:107:112:117) cm.
36(38:40:42:44:46) in.

Length
63(64:65:66:67:68) cm.
24¾(25:25½:26:26¼:26¾) in.

Sleeve Seam
56 cm.
22 in.

TENSION

32 sts. and 60 rows = 10 cm. (4 in.) square over sl. st. patt. on 2¾mm. needles. If your tension square does not correspond to these measurements, adjust the needle size used.

ABBREVIATIONS

k.=knit; p.=purl; st(s).=stitch(es); inc.= increase; dec.=decrease; beg.=begin(ning); rem. = remain(ing); rep. = repeat; alt. = alternate; tog. = together; sl. = slip stitch (transfer one stitch from left needle, knitwise unless otherwise stated, to right hand needle.); cont. = continue; patt. = pattern; foll. = following; folls. = follows; mm. = millimetres; cm. = centimetres; in. = inch(es); st.st. = stocking stitch.

BACK

Cast on 152(160:168:176:184:192) sts. with 2mm. needles and A, using thumb method. Work 5 cm. (2 in.) in k.1, p.1, rib. Change to 2¾mm. needles and patt. (N.B.: always sl. sts. purlwise. Do not pull yarn tightly when slipping sts.)
1st row (right side): with B, k.3, * sl. 2 purlwise, k.2, rep. from * to last st., k.1.
2nd row: with B, p.3, * sl. 2, p.2, rep. from * to last st., p.1.
3rd row: with A, k. to end.

4th row: with C, p.1, * sl. 2, p.2, rep. from * to last 3 sts., sl. 2, p.1.
5th row: with C, k.1, * sl. 2, k.2, rep. from * to last 3 sts., sl. 2, k.1.
6th row: with A, p. to end.
These 6 rows form patt. (whole garment, excluding welts, is worked in this patt.)
Cont. in patt. until work measures 40 cm. (15¾ in.)

Shape Armholes

Cast off 6(7:8:9:10:11) sts. at beg. of next 2 rows.
Dec. 1 st. at each end of next and foll. alt. rows until 116(120:126:130:134:138) sts. rem.
Work straight until armhole measures 21(22:23:24:25:26) cm. (8¼(8½:9:9½:9¾: 10¼) in.) on the straight.

Shape Shoulders

Cast off 4 sts. at beg. of next 14(12:8:6:4:2) rows.
Cast off 5 sts. at beg. of next 2(4:8:10:12: 14) rows.
Leave rem. 50(52:54:56:58:60) sts. on a spare needle.

FRONT

Work as for back until armhole measures 15(16:17:18:19:20) cm. (6(6¼:6¾:7:7½:7¾) in.) on the straight, ending with a wrong side row.

Shape Neck

1st row: patt. 49(50:52:53:54:55) sts., turn and leave rem. sts. on a spare needle. Dec. 1 st. at neck edge on next and every foll. alt. row until 33(34:36:37:38:39) sts. rem. Work straight until front matches back to shoulder, ending at armhole edge.

Shape Shoulder

Cast off 4 sts. at beg. of next and every alt. row 7(6:4:3:2:1) times more.
Cast off 5 sts. at beg. of alt. rows 1(2:4:5: 6:7) times.
Slip centre 18(20:22:24:26:28) sts. onto a holder.
Rejoin yarn to rem. 49(50:52:53:54:55) sts. and complete other side of neck to match, reversing shapings.

SLEEVES

Cast on 74(74:78:78:78:82) sts. with 2mm. needles and A.
Work 10 cm. (4 in.) in k.1, p.1 rib, ending with a right side row.
Inc. row (wrong side): p.4(4:6:6:6:8), * p. twice into next st., p.12, rep. from *, ending last rep. p.4(4:6:6:6:8). [80(80:84:84:84: 88) sts.]

Change to 2¾mm. needles and cont. in patt. as for back, inc. 1 st. at each end of 13th and every foll. 14th(12th:12th:10th: 10th:10th) row until there are 118(122:126: 130:134:138) sts.
Work straight until sleeve measures 56 cm. (22 in.).

Shape Top

Cast off 6(7:8:9:10:11) sts. at beg. of next 2 rows.
Dec. 1 st. at each end of every alt. row until 88 sts. rem.
Dec. 1 st. at each end of every foll. 3rd row until 60 sts. rem.
Dec. 1 st. at each end of every row until 44 sts. rem.
Cast off 4 sts. at beg. of next 6 rows.
Cast off rem. 20 sts.

NECKBAND

Sew up shoulder seams.
With set of 4 2mm. double-pointed needles and A, and with right side facing, k.50(52:54:56:58:60) sts. from back to neck, k. up 38 sts. down left side of neck, k.18 (20:22:24:26:28) sts. from centre front neck, k. up 38 sts. up right side of neck. [144(148:152:156:160:164) sts.]
Work in rounds in k.1, p.1, rib until neckband measures 6 cm. (2½ in.).
Cast off loosely in rib.

MAKING UP

Sew up side and sleeve seams.
Sew sleeve top into armhole.
Fold neckband in half and hem cast off edge to wrong side of neck.
Press on wrong side.

Cotton Sweater with Ribbed Yoke 1938

Waist-length sweater with narrow rib rollover collar, rib yoke pattern and welts, set-in sleeves, main part knitted in stocking stitch

★ Suitable for beginners

MATERIALS

Yarn
Pingouin Fil d'Ecosse No. 5
8(8:9) × 50g. balls

Needles
1 pair 2¼mm.
1 pair 2¾mm.

MEASUREMENTS

Bust
87(92:97) cm.
34(36:38) in.

Length
45(46:47) cm.
17¾(18:18½) in.

Sleeve Seam
46 cm.
18 in.

TENSION

31 sts. and 44 rows = 10 cm. (4 in.) square over stocking stitch on 2¾mm. needles. If your tension square does not correspond to these measurements, adjust the needle size used.

ABBREVIATIONS

k.=knit; p.=purl; st(s).=stitch(es); inc.= increase; dec.=decrease; beg.=begin(ning); rem. = remain(ing); rep. = repeat; alt. = alternate; tog. = together; sl. = slip stitch (transfer one stitch from left needle, knit-wise unless otherwise stated, to right hand needle.); cont. = continue; patt. = pattern; foll. = following; folls. = follows; mm. = millimetres; cm. = centimetre(s); in. = inch(es); st.st. = stocking stitch.

FRONT

Cast on 122(130:138) sts. with 2¼mm. needles and work in rib:
1st row (right side): k.2, * p.2, k.2, rep. from * to end.
2nd row: p.2, * k.2, p.2, rep. from * to end.
Rep. these 2 until work measures 5 cm. (2 in.), ending with a 2nd row, but inc. 1 st. in centre of last row.
Change to 2¾mm. needles and beg. with a k. row, work in st.st., inc. 1 st. at each

end of every foll. 8th row until there are 139(147:155) sts.
Cont. without shaping until work measures 24 cm. (9½ in.) from beg., ending with a p. row.

Shape Yoke Pattern
1st row: k.69(73:77), p.1, k.69(73:77).
2nd row: p.68(72:76), k.3, p.68(72:76).
3rd row: k.67(71:75), then for yoke k.2, p.1, k.2, then k.67(71:75).
4th row: p.66(70:74), k.1, p.1, k.3, p.1, k.1, p.66(70:74).
5th row: k.65(69:73), (p.1, k.3) twice, p.1, k.65(69:73).
6th row: p.64(68:72), (k.3, p.1) twice, k.3, p.64(68:72).
7th row: k.63(67:71), then k.2, (p.1, k.3) twice, p.1, k.2, then k.63(67:71).
8th row: p.62(66:70), k.1, (p.1, k.3) 3 times, p.1, k.1, p.62(66:70).

9th row: k.61(65:69), (p.1, k.3) 4 times, p.1, k.61(65:69).
10th row: p.60(64:68), (k.3, p.1) 4 times, k.3, p.60(64:68).
Cont. in this way, working 1 extra st. in patt. at each side of yoke on every row until 16 yoke rows have been worked.
NOTE: On right side rows where yoke begins and ends k.2, these sts. must be considered as part of yoke.

Shape Armholes
Cont. shaping yoke while shaping arm-hole. Cast off 3 sts. at beg. of next 8 rows, 2 sts. at beg. of next 2(4:6) rows and dec. 1 st. at both ends of every alt. row 10 times. [91(95:99) sts.]
During armhole dec., yoke patt. will reach armhole edge. Yoke patt. rows will read as folls.:
*** *1st row* (right side): k.1(3:1), * p.1, k.3,

rep. from * to last 2(4:2) sts., p.1, k.1(3:1).
2nd row: k.3(1:3), * p.1, k.3, rep. from * to last 4(2:4) sts., p.1, k.3(1:3). ***
Cont. in this patt. until work measures 39(40:41) cm. (15¼(15¾:16) in.) from beg., ending with a wrong side row.

Shape Neck and Shoulders
1st row: patt. 38(40:42) sts. and leave these sts. (left front) on spare needle; cast off next 15 sts., patt. to end. Cont. patt. on 38(40:42) sts. rem. for right front.
Work 1 row straight.
** Cast off 3 sts. at beg. of next row, 2 sts. at same edge on next 5 alt. rows and 1 st. on next 7 alt. rows, thus ending at side edge. [18(20:22) sts.]
Keeping neck edge straight, cast off 6 sts. at beg. of next and the foll. alt. row, for shoulder.
Work 1 row then cast off rem. 6(8:10) sts. **
With wrong side facing rejoin yarn to neck edge of left front sts.
Complete as for right front from ** to **.

BACK

Work as for front until side incs. are com-pleted, then cont. on 139(147:155) sts. in st.st. until work matches front to arm-holes, ending with a p. row.

Shape Armhole
Cast off 3 sts. at beg. of next 8 rows, 2 sts. at beg. of next 2(4:6) rows, and dec. 1 st. at both ends of every alt. row 10 times, ending with a p. row. [91(95:99) sts.]
Now work from *** to *** across all sts. without shaping until armholes measure same as front, ending with a wrong side row.

Shape Neck and Shoulders
1st row: cast off 6 sts., patt. until there are 22(24:26) sts. on right needle, leave on spare needle or holder for right back, cast off 35 sts., patt. to end.
Cont. on these 28(30:32) sts. for left back.
Cast off 6 sts. at beg. of next row and 5 sts. at neck edge on foll. row. Rep. last 2 rows once.
Cast off rem. 6(8:10) sts.
With wrong side facing rejoin yarn to neck edge of right back sts., cast off 5 sts., patt. to end.
Cast off 6 sts. at beg. of next row and 5 sts. at neck edge on foll. row. Cast off rem. 6(8:10) sts.

SLEEVES

Cast on 62(66:70) sts. with 2¼mm. needles and work in rib as for front welt for 7 cm. (2¾ in.), ending with a 2nd row. Change to 2¾mm. needles and beg. with a k. row work in st.st., inc. 1 st. at both ends of every foll. 8th row 20 times.
Cont. on 102(106:110) sts. until work measures 46 cm. (18 in.) from beg.

Shape Top
Cast off 3 sts. at beg. of next 8 rows, 2 sts. at beg. of next 2(4:6) rows, 1 st. at beg. of next 20(24:28) rows, 2 sts. at beg. of next 8(6:4) rows and 4 sts. at beg. of next 2 rows.
Cast off rem. 30 sts.

COLLAR
Sew up right shoulder seam, matching patt. and backstitching this and all seams. With right side of work facing, pick up and k. 143 sts., with 2¾mm. needles, all round neck edge. Work in yoke patt., as given for small size, for 10 cm. (4 in.). Cast off loosely in patt.

MAKING UP
Sew up left shoulder seam, cont. seam along collar for 2 cm. (¾ in.) then join remainder of seam on reverse side, fold collar over.
Sew in sleeves.
Sew up side and sleeve seams.
Press all seams lightly on wrong side with warm iron and damp cloth.

Silky Cotton Cardigan

1953

Casual cardigan with deep armholes and dropped shoulderline, in garter stitch rib with round neck and ribbed welts

★ Suitable for beginners

MATERIALS

Yarn
Phildar Perle 5
9(9:10:10:10) × 50g. balls

Needles
1 pair 2mm.
1 pair 2¾mm.

Buttons
7

MEASUREMENTS

Bust
82(87:92:97:102) cm.
32(34:36:38:40) in.

Length
55(56:57:58:59) cm.
21½(22:22¼:22¾:23¼) in.

Sleeve Seam
42(43:44:45:46) cm.
16½(16¾:17¼:17¾:18) in.

TENSION

28 sts. and 48 rows = 10 cm. (4 in.) square over patt. on 2¾mm. needles. If your tension square does not correspond to these measurements, adjust the needle size used.

ABBREVIATIONS

k.=knit; p.=purl; st(s).=stitch(es); inc.= increase(ing); dec.=decreas(ing); beg.=

begin(ning); rem. = remain(ing); rep. = repeat; alt. = alternate; tog. = together; sl. = slip (transfer one stitch from left needle, knitwise unless otherwise stated, to right hand needle.); cont. = continue; patt. = pattern; foll. = following; folls. = follows; mm. = millimetres; cm. = centimetres; in. = inches; st. st. = stocking st.: one row k., one row p.; g. st. = garter st.: every row k.; incs. = increases; decs. = decreases.

BACK

Cast on 121(129:137:145:153) sts. with 2mm. needles.
Work in rib as folls.:
1st rib row (right side): k.1, * p.1, k.1, rep. from * to end.
2nd rib row: p.1, * k.1, p.1, rep. from * to end.
Rep. last 2 rows for 5 cm. (2 in.), ending with a 2nd row and inc. 1 st. in last row. [122(130:138:146:154) sts.]
Change to 2¾mm. needles and work in patt. as folls.:
1st row (right side): k.2, * p.2, k.2, rep. from * to end.
2nd row: as 1st.
These 2 rows form patt.
Work straight in patt. until back measures 34 cm. (13¼ in.), ending with a wrong side row.

Shape Armholes
Cast off 5 sts. at beg. of next 2 rows. [112(120:128:136:144) sts.]
Work straight in patt. until armholes measure 21(22:23:24:25) cm. (8¼(8½: 9:9½:9¾) in.), ending with a wrong side row.

Shape Shoulders
Cast off 5(6:6:7:7) sts. at beg. of next 12(8:14:6:12) rows.
Cast off 6(5:0:6:6) sts. at beg. of next 2(6:0:8:2) rows.
Cast off rem. 40(42:44:46:48) sts.

LEFT FRONT

Cast on 70(74:78:82:86) sts. with 2mm. needles.

Work in rib as folls.:

1st row (right side): * k.1, p.1, rep. from * to last 2 sts., k.2.

2nd row: p.2, * k.1, p.1, rep. from * to end.

Rep. last 2 rows for 5 cm. (2 in.), ending with a 2nd row.

Change to 2¾mm. needles and work in patt. as for back until front matches back to armhole, ending with a wrong side row.

Shape Armhole

Cast off 5 sts. at beg. of next row. [65(69:73:77:81) sts.]

Work straight in patt. until armhole measures 15(16:17:18:19) cm. (5¾(6¼: 6½:7:7½) in.), ending with a right side row.

Shape Neck

Next row: cast off 9(10:9:10:9) sts., patt. to end.

Work 1 row.

Cast off 3 sts. at beg. of next and 4(4:5:5:6) foll. alt. rows.

Work 1 row.

Dec. 1 st. at neck edge on next and 4(4:3:3:2) foll. alt. rows. [36(39:42:45:48) sts.]

Work straight in patt. until front matches back to shoulder, ending with a wrong side row.

Shape Shoulder

Cast off 5(6:6:7:7) sts. at beg. of next and 5(3:6:2:5) foll. alt. rows.

Work 1(1:0:1:1) row.

Cast off 6(5:0:6:6) sts. at beg. of next and

0(2:0:3:0) foll. alt. rows.

Mark position of buttons on left front, first to come 2 cm. (¾ in.) from cast-on edge, then allowing for last on the 6th row of neckborder, space rem. 5 evenly between.

RIGHT FRONT

Cast on 70(74:78:82:86) sts. with 2mm. needles, and work in rib as folls.:

1st row (right side): k.2, * p.1, k.1, rep. from * to end.

2nd row: * p.1, k.1, rep. from * to last 2 sts., p.2.

Work to match left front reversing all shapings and making buttonholes as folls.:

1st buttonhole row (right side): work 6, cast off 3 sts., work to end.

2nd buttonhole row: work across, casting on 3 sts. over those cast off on previous row.

SLEEVES

Cast on 61(63:65:69:73) sts. with 2mm. needles.

Work in rib as for back, ending with a 2nd rib row, and inc. 1(3:1:1:1) sts. in last row. [62(66:66:70:74) sts.]

Change to 2¾mm. needles.

Work in patt. as for back, AT THE SAME TIME shaping sides as folls.:

1st and 2nd sizes:

Inc. 1 st. at each end of every 5th row 20(21) times, taking inc. sts. into patt.

Now inc. 1 st. at each end of every foll. 7th row until there are 116(122) sts.

3rd, 4th and 5th sizes:

Inc. 1 st. at each end of every 5th row

until there are 128(134:140) sts., taking inc. sts. into patt.

All sizes:

[116(122:128:134:140) sts.]

Work straight in patt., until sleeve measures 44(45:46:47:48) cm. (17¼(17¾: 18:18½:18¾) in.).

Cast off loosely.

NECKBORDER

Sew up shoulders.

With right side facing and 2mm. needles, k. up 43(45:47:49:51) sts. up right side of neck, 51(55:57:59:61) sts. across back neck and 43(45:47:49:51) sts. down left side of neck. [137(145:151:157:163) sts.]

Work in rib as folls.:

1st row (wrong side): p.2, * k.1, p.1, rep. from * to last st., p.1.

2nd row: k.2, * p.1, k.1, rep. from * to last st., k.1.

Rep. last 2 rows once more, then 1st row again.

6th row: rib 6, cast off 3 sts., rib to end.

7th row: work back, casting on 3 sts. over those cast off on previous row.

Work 6 more rows in rib.

Cast off evenly in rib.

MAKING UP

Place centre of cast-off edge of sleeves to shoulders.

Sew in position sewing to front and back at underarm.

Sew up side and sleeve seams.

Sew on buttons.

Luxurious Fair Isle Cardigan

Round-neck silky cardigan, with seven-colour Fair Isle pattern on yoke and cuffs, and ribbed welts

★★ Suitable for knitters with some previous experience

MATERIALS

Yarn

Maxwell Cartledge Pure Silk
7(7:7:7:7:7) × 50g. balls (Main Col A)
1(1:1:1:1:1) × 50g. ball each of Contrast Cols. B, C, D, E, F, G, H.

Needles

1 pair 3mm.
1 pair 3¼mm.
1 pair 3½mm.

Buttons

6

MEASUREMENTS

Bust

82(87:92:97:102:107) cm.
32(34:36:38:40:42) in.

Length

55(55:57:57:58:60) cm.
21½(21½:22¼:22¼:22¾:23½) in.

Sleeve Seam

44 cm.
17¼ in.

TENSION

30 sts. and 36 rows = 10 cm. (4 in.) square over st.st. on 3¼mm. needles. If your tension square does not correspond to these

Dec. 1 st. at each end of every row 9(13:14: 18:22:22) times. [95(95:99:99:99:107) sts.]
Cont. in st.st. until armhole measures 19(19: 20:20:20:21) cm. (7½(7½:7¾:7¾:7¾:8¼) in.)

Shape Shoulders

Cast off 10(10:10:10:10:13) sts. at beg. of next 4(4:2:2:2:2) rows.
Cast off 11 sts. at beg. of next 2(2:4:4:4:4) rows.
Leave rem. 33(33:35:35:35:37) sts. on spare needle or st. holder for neckband.

RIGHT FRONT

Cast on 59(63:67:71:75:79) sts. with 3mm. needles and A.
Work in rib as for back for 6 cm. (2¼ in.).
Change to 3¼mm. needles and work in st.st. until front measures same as back to armhole shaping, ending at armhole edge.

Shape Armhole

Next row: cast off 8 sts., p. to end.
Dec. 1 st. at armhole edge on every row 9(13: 13:17:21:25) times. [42(42:44:44:44:48) sts.]
1st and 2nd sizes only: p.1 row.
Change to 3½mm. needles.
All sizes now have right side facing.
Work 27 rows from chart, working the 12 st. rep. 3(3:3:3:3:4) times across row and odd sts. as marked on chart.
Change to 3¼mm. needles.
Cont. in st.st. until armhole measures 11(11: 13:13:13:14) cm. (4¼(4¼:5:5:5:5½) in.), ending at neck edge.

Shape Neck

Next row: cast off 2(2:1:1:1:3) sts., k. to end.
Dec. 1 st. at neck edge on every row 10(10:11:11:11:11) times.
Cont. without shaping until armhole measures same as back to shoulder shaping, ending at armhole edge.

Shape Shoulder

1st row: cast off 10(10:10:10:10:11) sts., p. to end.
2nd row: k.
3rd row: cast off 10(10:11:11:11:11) sts., p. to end.
4th row: k.
Cast off rem. sts.

LEFT FRONT

Work as for right front, reversing shapings.

SLEEVES

Cast on 64(64:68:68:68:70) sts. with 3mm. needles and A.
Work in rib as for back for 5 cm. (2 in.), increasing 14(14:18:18:18:20) sts. evenly across last row. [78(78:86:86:86:90) sts.]
Change to 3¼mm. needles.
Work in st.st. for 2 cm. (¾ in.).
Change to 3½mm. needles and work 27 rows from chart as marked on chart for sleeves, working 12 st. rep. 6(6:7:7:7:7) times across row and odd sts. as marked on chart.
Change to 3¼mm. needles and inc. 1 st. at each end of next and every foll. 6th row until there are 92(92:96:96:96:98) sts.
Cont. without shaping until sleeve measures 44 cm. (17¼ in.).

Shape Top

Dec. 1 st. at each end of every alt. row 18(18:21:21:21:22) times.
Cast off 2 sts. at beg. of next 12(12:10:10:10: 10) rows. Cast off rem. 32(32:34:34:34:34) sts.

NECKBAND

Sew up shoulder seams.
With right side facing, 3mm. needles and A, pick up and k.31 sts. from right neck, k.33(33:35:35:35:37) sts. from back holder or spare needle, pick up and k.31 sts. from left front. [95(95:97:97:97:99) sts.]
Work 8 rows in k.1, p.1 rib.
Cast off in rib.

LEFT BORDER

With 3mm. needles and A, pick up and k.164 sts. evenly along left front.
Work 7 rows in k.1, p.1 rib.
Cast off in rib.

RIGHT BORDER

With 3mm. needles and A, pick up and k.164 sts. evenly along right front.
Work 3 rows in k.1, p.1 rib.
Next row: rib 4 sts., * cast off 3 sts., rib 22, rep. from * to last 4 sts., rib 4.
Next row: rib 4 sts., * cast on 3 sts., rib 23, rep. from * to last 4 sts., rib 4.
Work 2 rows in rib.
Cast off in rib.

MAKING UP

Sew up side and sleeve seams.
Set in sleeves.
Sew on buttons opposite buttonholes.
Press lightly with a damp cloth.

measurements, adjust the needle size used.

ABBREVIATIONS

k.=knit; p.=purl; st(s).=stitch(es); inc.= increase; dec.=decrease; beg.=begin(ning); rem. = remain(ing); rep. = repeat; alt. = alternate; tog. = together; sl. = slip stitch (transfer one stitch from left needle, knit-wise unless otherwise stated, to right hand needle.); cont. = continue; patt. = pattern; foll. = following; folls. = follows; mm. = millimetres; cm. = centimetres; in. = inch(es); st.st. = stocking stitch.

BACK

Cast on 129(137:143:151:159:167) sts. with 3mm. needles and A.
1st row: k.1, * p.1, k.1, rep. from * to end.
2nd row: p.1, * k.1, p.1, rep. from * to end.
Rep. these 2 rows for 6 cm. (2¼ in.).
Change to 3¼mm. needles and st.st.
Work until back measures 36(36:37:37:38: 38) cm. (14(14:14½:14½:15:15) in.)

Shape Armholes

Cast off 8 sts. at beg. of next 2 rows.

27 rows

← 12 st. patt. rep.→
← 6th right front size→ ☐ A
3rd, 4th and 5th sleeve ☑ B
sizes ◪ C
1st and 2nd right front sizes ◙ D
← and 1st, 2nd and 6th sleeve → ⊡ E
sizes ☒ F
← 3rd, 4th and 5th right front sizes → ☑ G
◪ H

Sweater with Peter Pan Collar

1981

Reverse stocking stitch sweater with set-in sleeves, garter stitch collar, cuffs and welts, and zip or button closing

★★ Suitable for knitters with some previous experience

MATERIALS

Yarn
Maxwell Cartlidge Shanghai
6(6:7:7) × 50g. balls

Needles
1 pair 2¾mm.
1 pair 3¼mm.
1 3mm. crochet hook (for button version)

Buttons
2

OR

Zip
1 10 cm. (4 in.)

MEASUREMENTS

Bust
82(87:92:97) cm.
32(34:36:38) in.

Length
54(55:58:59) cm.
21¼(21½:22¾:23¼) in.

Sleeve Seam
44(44:45:45) cm.
17¼(17¼:17¾:17¾) in.

TENSION

25 sts. and 32 rows = 10 cm. (4 in.) square over st. st. on 3¼mm. needles. If your tension square does not correspond to these measurements, adjust the needle size used.

ABBREVIATIONS

k.=knit; p.=purl; st(s).=stitch(es); inc.= increas(ing); dec.=decreas(ing); beg.= begin(ning); rem. = remain(ing); rep. = repeat; alt. = alternate; tog. = together; sl. = slip (transfer one stitch from left needle, knitwise unless otherwise stated, to right hand needle.); cont. = continue; patt. = pattern; foll. = following; folls. = follows; mm. = millimetres; cm. = centimetres; in. = inches; st. st. = stocking st.: one row k., one row p.; g. st. = garter st.: every row k.; incs. = increases; decs. = decreases; m.1 = make 1 st.: pick up horizontal loop lying before next st. and k. into the back of it.

FRONT

** Cast on 99(105:111:117) sts. with 2¾mm. needles.

Work 11 rows in g. st.
Change to 3¼mm. needles and reverse st. st. (p.1 row, k.1 row alternately, having p. side as right side).
Work 12 rows.
Dec. 1 st. at each end of next row, and then every 6th row until 91(97:103:109) sts. rem.
Work 9 rows.
Inc. 1 st. at each end of next row, and then every 8th row until there are 105(111:117:123) sts.
Work until front measures 36(36:38:38) cm. (14(14:15:15) in.) from beg., ending with a k. row.

Shape Armholes

Cast off 4(4:5:5) sts. at beg. of next 2 rows.
Now dec. 1 st. at each end of every row until 91(93:97:99) sts. rem., and then every alt. row until 85(87:91:93) sts. rem. **
Work until armholes measure 14(15:15:16) cm. (5½(5¾:5¾:6¼) in.) measured on the straight, ending with a p. row.

Shape Neck

Next row: k.37(38:40:41) sts., cast off 11 sts., k. to end.
Cont. on last set of sts.
Dec. 1 st. at neck edge on next 6(6:6:6) rows, and then the 3(3:4:4) foll. alt. rows, ending at armhole edge.

Shape Shoulder

Dec. at neck edge on foll. alt. rows twice more, and at the same time cast off 7(6:7:7) sts. at beg. of next row, and 6(7:7:7) sts. at beg. of 2 foll. alt. rows.
Work 1 row.
Cast off rem. 7(7:7:8) sts.
Rejoin yarn to rem. sts. at neck edge and complete to match first side, working one extra row before shaping shoulder.

BACK

Work as for front from ** to **.
Work until armholes measure 10(10:11:12) cm. (4(4:4¼:4¾) in.) measured on the straight, ending with a p. row.

Divide for Back Opening

Next row: k.42(43:45:46) sts., cast off 1 st., k. to end.
Cont. on last set of sts.
Work until armhole measures same as front, ending at armhole edge.

Shape Shoulder

Cast off at beg. of next and foll. alt. rows 7(6:7:7) sts. once, 6(7:7:7) sts. twice, and 7(7:7:8) sts. once.

Work 1 row.
Cast off rem. 16(16:17:17) sts.
Rejoin yarn to rem. sts. at opening edge and complete to match first side.

SLEEVES

Cast on 53(53:55:57) sts. with 3¼mm. needles.
Work 10 rows in reverse st. st.
Cont. in reverse st. st., inc. 1 st. at each end of next row, and then every 6th row until there are 61(63:73:77) sts., and then every 8th row until there are 75(77:81:85) sts.
Work until sleeve measures 44(44:45:45) cm. (17¼(17¼:17¾:17¾) in.) from beg., ending with a k. row.

Shape Top

Cast off 4(4:5:5) sts. at beg. of next 2 rows.
Now dec. 1 st. at each end of every row until 57(59:61:63) sts. rem., then every alt. row until 33(33:33:35) sts. rem., and then every row until 19(19:19:21) sts. rem.
Cast off.

COLLAR

Cast on 43(43:45:47) sts. with 2¾mm. needles.
Work 6 rows in g. st.
Next row: k.2, m.1, k. to last 2 sts., m.1, k.2.
Working in g. st., cont. to inc. in this way at each end of every 6th row until there are 51(51:53:55) sts.
Work 5 rows.
Cast off.
Work other side of collar to match.

CUFFS

Cast on 53(53:55:57) sts. with 2¾mm. needles.

Work 6 rows in g. st.
Next row: k.2, m.1, k. to last 2 sts., m.1, k.2.
Working in g. st., cont. to inc. in this way at each end of every 6th row until there are 61(61:63:65) sts.
Work 5 rows.
Cast off.
Work another cuff to match.

MAKING UP

With wrong side facing, block each piece and press lightly with a warm iron and damp cloth.
Sew up shoulder, side and sleeve seams.
Set in sleeves.
Sew cast-on edges of collar pieces to neck edge from back opening to centre front crochet along back opening edges, making 2 small button loops.
Sew on buttons.
Sew cast-on edges of cuffs to sleeve edges.
Press seams lightly.

Roll-collar Cotton Sweater   1981

Short cotton sweater in stocking stitch with elbow-length raglan sleeves and narrow rollover collar

★ Suitable for beginners

MATERIALS

Yarn
Twilleys Pegasus Cotton
4(4:5) × 100g. balls

Needles
1 pair 5mm.
1 pair 6½mm.
1 circular 6½mm.

MEASUREMENTS

Bust
87(92:97) cm.
34(36:38) in.

Length
54(57:60) cm.
21¼(22¼:23¾) in.

Sleeve Seam
18 cm.
7 in.

TENSION

8 sts. and 10 rows = 6 cm. (2¼ in.) square over st. st. on 6½mm. needles. If your tension square does not correspond to these measurements, adjust the needle size used.

ABBREVIATIONS

k.=knit; p.=purl; st(s).=stitch(es); inc.= increas(ing); dec.=decreas(ing); beg.= begin(ning); rem. = remain(ing); rep. = repeat; alt. = alternate; tog. = together; sl. = slip (transfer one stitch from left needle to right hand needle.); cont. = continue; patt. = pattern; foll. = following; folls. = follows; mm. = millimetres; cm. = centimetres; in. = inches; st. st. = stocking st.: one row k., one row p.; g. st. = garter st.: every row k.; incs. = increases; decs. = decreases.

BACK

Cast on 58(58:62) sts. with 5mm. needles and work 9 rows in k.2, p.2 rib, inc. 0(1:1) st. at each end of last rib row and inc. 0(1:0) st. at centre of last rib row. [58(61:64) sts.]
Change to 6½mm. needles and cont. in st. st. until work measures 36(37:38) cm. (14(14½:15) in.) from beg., ending with a p. row.

Shape Raglans
Cast off 4 sts. at beg. of next 2 rows. [50(53:56) sts.]
Next row: k.2, k.2 tog., k. to last 4 sts., k.2 tog., k.2.
Next row: p. **
Rep. these 2 rows until 22(21:22) sts. rem.
Leave sts. on a spare needle.

FRONT

Work as for back to **
Rep. these 2 rows until 30(29:30) sts. rem., ending with a right side row.

Shape Neck
1st row: p. 9 sts., turn.
Cont. to shape raglan as set on back and dec. 1 st. at neck edge on every right side row until 1 st. rem.
Fasten off.
Sl. centre 12(11:12) sts. onto a spare needle to be worked later as collar.
Rejoin yarn to rem. sts. and complete as for 1st side, reversing all shapings.

SLEEVES

Cast on 38(42:46) sts. with 5mm. needles and work 9 rows in k.2, p.2 rib, (for first and second sizes only, inc. 1 st. at each

end of last rib row). [40(44:46) sts.]
Change to 6½mm. needles and work in st. st., but inc. 1 st. at each end of 12th row. [42(46:48) sts.]
Cont. until work measures 18 cm. (7 in.) from beg., ending with a p. row.

Shape Raglans

Cast off 2 sts. at beg. of next 2 rows.
Next row: k.2, k.2 tog., k. to last 4 sts., k.2 tog., k.2.
Next row: p.
Rep. these 2 rows until 10 sts. rem.

Leave sts. on a spare needle.

ROLL COLLAR

Press all pieces, avoiding rib, with a warm iron and damp cloth.
Sew up raglan edges of sleeves to those of front and back.
With right side facing, beg. at right back neck, using 6½mm. circular needle, k. across the 22(21:22) sts. of back neck, 10 sts. of left sleeve, pick up and k.6 sts. along left neck edge, k. across the

12(11:12) sts. of front neck, pick up and k.6 sts. along right neck and then k. across the 10 sts. of right sleeve. [66(64:66) sts.]
K. 16 rounds.
Cast off loosely: collar rolls over to show p. side.
Press all seams and collar on reverse side with warm iron and damp cloth.

MAKING UP

Sew up sleeve and side seams.

Stripe-bordered Cardigan

Thick cotton cardigan in two lengths, with set-in sleeves, round neck, buttonband, cuffs and hem in contrast stripes

★ Suitable for beginners

NB Short version photographed

MATERIALS

Yarn
Pingouin Coton Naturel 8 Fils
Short Cardigan:
9(10:10:11:11) × 50g. balls Main Col. A
2(2:2:2:2) × 50g. balls Col. B
Long Cardigan:
11(12:12:13:13) × 50g. balls Main Col. A
2(2:2:2:2) × 50g. balls Col. B

Needles
1 pair 3mm.
1 pair 3¾mm.
st. holders

Buttons
Short Cardigan:
8
Long Cardigan:
10

MEASUREMENTS

Bust
82(87:92:97:102) cm.
32(34:36:38:40) in.

Length
Short Cardigan:
58(59:59:60:60) cm.
22¾(23¼:23¼:23¾:23¾) in.
Long Cardigan:
71(72:72:73:73) cm.
27¾(28¼:28¼:28½:28½) in.

Sleeve Seam
43(44:45:45:46) cm.
16¾(17¼:17¾:17¾:18) in.

TENSION

23 sts. and 28 rows = 10 cm. (4 in.) square over st. st. on 3¾mm. needles. If your

tension square does not correspond to these measurements, adjust the needle size used.

ABBREVIATIONS

k. = knit; p. = purl; st(s). = stitch(es); inc. = increas(ing); dec. = decreas(ing); beg. = begin(ning); rem. = remain(ing); rep. = repeat; alt. = alternate; tog. = together; sl. = slip (transfer one stitch from left needle, knitwise unless otherwise stated, to right hand needle.); cont. = continue; patt. = pattern; foll. = following; folls. = follows; mm. = millimetres; cm. = centimetres; in. = inches; st. st. = stocking st.: one row k., one row p.; g. st. = garter st.: every row k.; incs. = increases; decs. = decreases.

NB Use yarn double throughout.

BACK

Cast on 103(109:115:121:127) sts. with 3mm. needles and A.
Work in stripe rib as folls.:
1st row: with A, * k.1, p.1, rep. from * to last st., k.1.
2nd row: with A, k.1, * k.1, p.1, rep. from * to last 2 sts., k.2.
3rd and 4th rows: as 1st and 2nd.
5th and 6th rows: with B, as 1st and 2nd.
These 6 rows form patt.
Cont. until 34 patt. rows have been worked.
Change to 3¾mm. needles and st. st.
With A, cont. until work measures 38 cm. (15 in.) for short version or 51 cm. (20 in.) for long version.

Shape Armholes

Cast off 5(6:6:7:8) sts. at beg. of next 2 rows.

Dec. 1 st. at each end of next 4 rows.
Dec. 1 st. at each end of next and every foll. alt. row until 75(77:79:81:83) sts. rem.
Cont. without shaping until work measures 48 cm. (18¾ in.) for short version or 61 cm. (24 in.) for long version.
Inc. 1 st. at each end of next and every foll. 6th row 4 times. [83(85:87:89:91) sts.]
Cont. without shaping until work measures 58(59:59:60:60) cm. (22¾:23¼:23¼:23¾:23¾) in.) for short version or 71(72:72:73:73) cm. (27¾:28¼:28¼:28½:28½) in.) for long version.

Shape Shoulders

Cast off 7 sts. at beg. of next 6 rows.
Cast off 5(6:6:7:7) sts. at beg. of next 2 rows.
Leave 31(31:33:33:35) sts. on holder.

POCKET LININGS

Short version only:
Cast on 31 sts. with 3mm. needles and A.
Work 33 rows in striped rib as for back.
Leave sts. on holder.
Fasten off.

LEFT FRONT

Short version:
Cast on 67(70:73:76:79) sts. with 3mm. needles and A.
Work 32 rows in striped rib as for back.
Pocket row: rib 6(8:8:10:12) sts., cast off 31 sts., rib 30(31:34:35:36).
34th row: rib to cast off section, rib across pocket lining, rib to end.
Long version:
Work as for short version, but work 34 rows in striped rib and omit pocket opening.
Both versions:
Change to 3¾mm. needles, with A work as folls.:

Next row: k.43(46:49:52:55) sts., turn, leave 24 sts. on holder for button band. Cont. in st. st. until work measures same as back to armhole, ending at side edge.

Shape Armhole
Cast off 5(6:6:7:8) sts. at beg. of next row.
Work 1 row.
Dec. 1 st. at armhole edge on next 4 rows.
Dec. 1 st. at armhole edge on next and foll. alt. rows until 29(30:31:32:33) sts. rem.
Cont. without shaping until work measures 48 cm. (18¾ in.) for short version or 61 cm. (24 in.) for long version.
Inc. 1 st. at armhole edge on next and every foll. 6th row 4 times in all, AT THE SAME TIME, when work measures 53(54:54:55:55) cm. (20¾(21¼:21¼: 21½: 21½) in.) for short version or 66(67:67: 68:68) cm. (26(26¼:26¼: 26¾:26¾) in.) for long version, work as folls.:

Shape Neck
Dec. 1 st. at neck edge on next 4 rows.
Dec. 1 st. at neck edge on next and foll. alt. rows until 26(27:27:28:28) sts. rem.
Cont. until work measures same as back to shoulder shaping, ending at armhole edge.

Shape Shoulder
Cast off 7 sts. at beg. of next and foll. 2 alt. rows.
Work 1 row.
Cast off.

BUTTON BAND
Rejoin yarns to 24 sts. on holder and with 3mm. needles, work in striped rib as for back until band measures same as work to neck shaping when slightly stretched, ending with 2 rows of B.
Leave sts. on holder.
Fasten off.
Sew in place.

Mark positions for buttons evenly along band, first to come 1 cm. (½ in.) from lower edge of band, last to be worked on third and fourth rows from top of band, and rem. buttons spaced evenly between.

RIGHT FRONT
Work as for left front, reversing all shapings and pocket row. Work button-holes to correspond with positions marked on left front for buttons, each hole to be worked as folls.:
1st buttonhole row (right side): rib 10, cast off 3 sts., rib to end.
2nd buttonhole row: rib, casting on 3 sts. over those cast off.

SLEEVES
Cast on 51(53:55:57:59) sts. with 3mm. needles and A.
Work 33 rows in stripe patt. as for back.
34th row: rib 4(1:3:3:4), * inc. 1 st., rib 5(6:6:6:6) sts., rep. from * 6 times more, inc. 1 st., rib 4(2:2:4:5) sts. [59(61:63: 65:67) sts.]
Change to 3¾mm. needles and with A, work in st. st., inc. 1 st. at each end of every 7th row until there are 83(85:87: 89:91) sts.
Cont. without shaping until work measures 43(44:45:45:46) cm. (16¾(17¼: 17¾:17¾:18) in.)

Shape Top
Cast off 5(6:6:7:8) sts. at beg. of next 2 rows.
Dec. 1 st. at each end of next 4 rows.
Dec. 1 st. at each end of foll. alt. rows until 39 sts. rem.
Cast off 3 sts. at beg. of next 8 rows.
Cast off.

NECKBAND
Sew up shoulder seams.
With 3mm. needles and A, rib across right front band, pick up and k. 15(16:17:18:19) sts. from right front neck, k. across back neck sts. from holder, pick up and k. 15(16:17:18:19) sts. across left front neck and rib across 24 sts. of button band. [109(111:115:117:121) sts.]
Work 3 rows in rib.
Cast off in rib.

MAKING UP
Sew up side and sleeve seams.
Set in sleeves.
Sew down pocket linings (short version).
Press lightly, excluding ribbing, with warm iron over damp cloth.
Sew on buttons.

Thigh-length Silk Coolie Coat 1934

Straight coat in linen stitch, with wide, cuffed, set-in sleeves, straight collar in moss stitch, and patch pockets

★ Suitable for beginners

MATERIALS

Yarn
Maxwell Cartlidge Shanghai
13(14:15:16) × 50g. balls

Needles
1 pair 4mm.
1 pair 5½mm.

Buttons
1

MEASUREMENTS

Bust
82(87:92:97) cm.
32(34:36:38) in.

Length
72(74:75:76) cm.
28¼(29:29½:29¾) in.

Sleeve Seam (with cuff turned up)
45 cm.
17¾ in.

TENSION

11½ sts. and 15 rows = 5 cm. (2 in.) square over pattern on 5½mm. needles, using DOUBLE yarn. If your tension square does not correspond to these measurements, adjust the needle size used.

ABBREVIATIONS

k.=knit; p.=purl; st(s).=stitch(es); inc.= increase; dec.=decrease; beg.=begin(ning); rem.=remain(ing); rep. = repeat; alt. = alternate; tog. = together; sl. = slip stitch (transfer one stitch from left needle, knitwise unless otherwise stated, to right hand needle.); cont. = continue; patt. = pattern; foll. = following; folls. = follows; mm. = millimetres; cm. = centimetre(s); in. = inch(es); sl.1 p. = slip one st. purlwise.
NOTE: Use two strands of yarn throughout.

BACK

Cast on 115(121:127:133) sts. with 4mm. needles.
Change to 5½mm. needles and patt.
1st row (wrong side): * k.1, sl.1p. with yarn at front, rep. from * to the last st., k.1.
2nd row: k.1, * p.1, sl.1p. with yarn at back, rep. from * to the last 2 sts., p.1, k.1.
These 2 rows form patt.
Work 21 more rows.
Dec. 1 st. at each end of next row, and then every 22nd row until 103(109: 115:121) sts. rem.
Work until back measures 51(51:52:52) cm. (20(20:20½:20½) in.) from beg., ending with a wrong side row (mark each end of last row to indicate start of armholes).

Shape Raglans

Dec. 1 st. at each end of every row until 89(95:97:103) sts. rem., and then every alt. row until 33(35:35:37) sts. rem., ending with a wrong side row.
Cast off.

LEFT FRONT.

** Cast on 61(63:67:69) sts. with 4mm. needles.
Change to 5½mm. needles and patt.
Work 23 rows.
Dec. 1 st. at side edge on next row, and then every 22nd row until 55(57:61:63) sts. rem.
Work until front measures same as back to armholes, ending with a wrong side row.
** (Mark end of last row to indicate start of armhole).

Shape Raglan

Dec.1 st. at armhole edge on every row until 48(50:52:54) sts. rem., and then every alt. row until 27(27:28:28) sts. rem., ending at front edge.

Shape Neck

Next row: cast off 8(8:9:9) sts., work to end.
Cont. to dec. for raglan on next and foll. alt. rows, and at the same time dec. 1 st. at neck edge on the next 6 rows, and then the 4 foll. alt. rows.
k.2 tog. and fasten off.

RIGHT FRONT

Follow instructions for left front from ** to ** having decreasings at opposite edge. (Mark beg. of last row to indicate start of armhole).

Shape Raglan

Dec. 1 st. at armhole edge on every row until 48(50:52:54) sts. rem., and then every alt. row until 27(27:28:28) sts. rem., ending at armhole edge.

Shape Neck

Next row: work to last 8(8:9:9) sts., cast off these sts. Break yarn.
Turn and rejoin yarn to rem. sts. at neck edge and complete to match left front.

SLEEVES

Cast on 51(53:55:57) sts. with 4mm. needles.
Change to 5½mm. needles and patt. as back.
Work 11 rows.
Inc. 1 st. at each end of next row, and then every 10th(9th:8th:8th) row until there are 75(79:83:87) sts.
Work until sleeve measures 44 cm. (17¼ in.) from beg., ending with a wrong side row. (Mark each end of last row to indicate start of sleeve top).
Work 2(2:4:4) more rows.

Shape Top

Dec. 1 st. at each end of next row, and then every alt. row until 11 sts. rem.
Work 1 row. Cast off.

COLLAR

Cast on 93(93:97:97) sts. with 4mm. needles.
1st row: k.2, * p.1, k.1, rep. from * to the last st., k.1.
2nd row: * k.1, p.1, rep. from * to the last st., k.1.
Rep. 1st and 2nd rows until collar measures 6.5 cm. (2½ in.) from beg., ending with 2nd row.
Change to 5½mm. needles and work 6.5 cm. (2½ in.) in patt., ending with 2nd row.
Cast off.

POCKETS (2)

Cast on 33 sts. with 4mm. needles.
Change to 5½mm. needles.
Work 15 cm. (5¾ in.) in patt. ending with 2nd row.
Cast off.

CUFFS (2)

Cast on 51(53:55:57) sts. with 4mm. needles.
Change to 5½mm. needles.
Work 11 cm. (4¼ in.) in patt., ending with 2nd row.
Cast off.

MAKING UP

Press each piece lightly on the wrong side with warm iron and damp cloth.
Sew cast off edge of cuffs to cast on edge of sleeves so that patt. is reversed.
Sew up raglan seams. Sew up side and sleeve seams, reversing the seam at cuffs.
Turn up cuff.
Sew pockets in position.
Sew cast on edge of collar to neck edge, leaving 1 cm. (½ in.) open for buttonhole at right side, starting 1 cm. (½ in.) from front edge.
Press seams lightly.
Sew on button.